THE RECKONING ANTHOLOGY

An examniation of black creativity and expression

Reckoning Publishing LLC

Copyright © 2020 Reckoning Publishing LLC

All rights reserved

No part of this book may be reproduced, or stored in a retrieval system, or transmitted in any form or by any means, electronic, mechanical, photocopying, recording, or otherwise, without express written permission of the publisher.

ISBN: 978-1-7355714-1-6

Printed in the United States of America

This anthology is dedicated to everyone who never fit the mold.

Caring for myself is not self-induglence, it is self-preservation, and that is an act of political warfare.

AUDRE LORDE

CONTENTS

Title Page	1
Copyright	2
Dedication	3
Epigraph	4
Alexis Lawson	7
Shakira Washington	35
Jazzmeen Underwood	101
Eddie White	107
Jada Sherffield	129
Paris Taylor	137

ALEXIS LAWSON

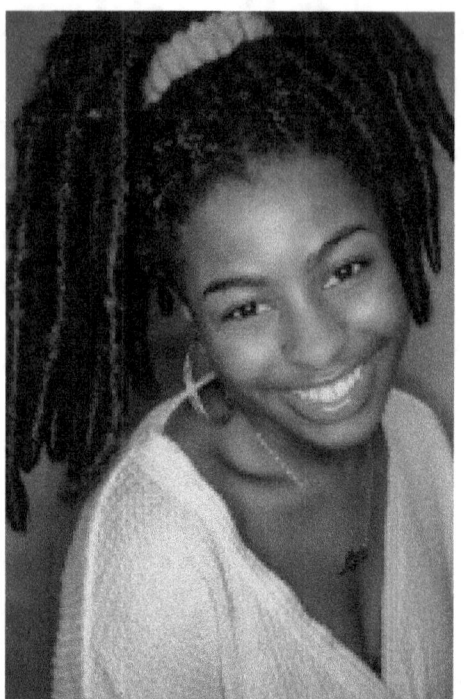

Alexis Lawson is a poet, storyteller, and author of the new poetry collection *The Beauty in my Bare Bones* (2019). Born and raised in Cleveland, Ohio, transplanted to North Carolina. Still residing in North Carolina, Alexis is an elementary school teacher by day, and spoken word poet by night. Alexis has a BA in creative writing from Appalachian State University. She is very passionate about making arts more accessible to the youth, while writing fiction through the black voice, incorporating her culture into narratives that some otherwise may not see representation. She enjoys exploring themes including self-love, black womanhood, reflection, and love, and connections.

A Train Ride to Nowhere

I began this journal the way I begin every other one. Date in the left hand corner with the time I started, following directly after. I pulled my feet onto the seat and made sure each earbud was snug in between my ears before I began.

I'm pretty sure I'm riddled with the lows of love. It's surrounded me my entire life. No representation, no model for me to look at. It's always, try hard, then try harder, and if you got a little fight left in you, try again. Never walk away when you are not respected, when the needs that you have expressed have continuously been neglected. I've always looked at love like a game of survival, like may the best one win. And now that I'm older, trying to work myself through the tangles of my upbringing, I know that love will not work off a basis of survival.

You see, my friends love to think that I have this unrealistic idea of what love is. But everything I want, I can equally provide. So, no, I won't settle for what rests at my feet, when I've asked them to meet me eye to eye.

My mama always told me to meet people where they were, and treat people how I wanted to be treated, and to always pick my shit up because I didn't have no maid. The words flew from her mouth the way she claimed they flew from my grandma's. Maybe it's been inscripted in the code of our DNA. The rule book on how to parent black. Because more often than not, my friends could tell the same stories I could and with no context needed, we just understood.

There was a lot of "stay in a child's place" and even more of "what happens in this house, stays in this house". And I know you should be grateful for the life that you have and the parents you were given, and don't get me wrong I am, but lord knows there are some things I wish I would've gotten a talk about instead of a lesson.

I sit in the same seat every day. Mainly because I get on the train right before the work rush. I missed the train one time and I was in a completely different world. Men dressing up, carrying leather briefcases with their top buttons undone, and ties hanging loosely around their necks. Women clinging to their purses as they gazed out the windows, as the rail lines blended into each other. There were no kids, no joyful greetings; they never sat next to the same person twice. Maybe saw them every morning, or even skipped them in line at the shop, on the platform, but never anything more.

Why is it such a horrible thing to want more with someone? Maybe the fear isn't wanting more, maybe the fear is not knowing what more intels.

Mr. Malone sits across from me every morning. The first time I rode this route by myself he said hello to me and the next day, and the one after that, and everyday after that until one day things were different. The power blew in my house, in the middle of the night, and didn't charge my phone. With no alarms, naturally I woke up late. I scrambled trying to find a shirt that wasn't too wrinkled from resting in its newfound home, the laundry basket. I'm pretty sure that was the day I wore two different shoes. I parked my car and I'm running. Running to the elevator, running through people to make it to the platform. Soon as I pushed past my last person, shoes untied, hair still in-bonnet, the train doors are beginning to close. I'm sure I never ran that fast in my life.

As my mom would say, I made it by the grace of God. I sit in the same seat I do every morning, panting and sweating from what feels like a 5k that I just ran.

Mr. Malone says, "Hello". I look up; unsure of how I appear, to him reaching out a white bag to me. Inside is an egg and cheese croissant with an orange juice and a metal straw. Still trying to catch what breath I had left, we made eye contact, and he nodded. That morning I didn't have time to stop at the shop and grab my breakfast, an egg and cheese croissant with orange juice.

Later that week, I said hello, expecting it to go no further than that, but something in me wanted more. I wanted to know how someone who says one word to me every morning, managed to remember my breakfast order down to the metal straw that I carry everywhere I go. So I asked; and he simply told me that every morning he sees me sitting on a bench for about 15 minutes before the train comes with a white bag and earbuds in, but that day he didn't. So he went into the shop and asked the cashier if he knew who I was. I believe his name was Marc, or something like that. He said he didn't know me but that I came in there every morning. He told me he asked him what I bought, and got it for me, just in case I was running a bit late. But that didn't explain the straw, so I asked. He said he had never seen me use anything else, so he grabbed one from the register for good measure. Now, every now and again our conversations extend from hello to what I'm writing or something like that, but sometimes they just stay at hello and that's fine.

I heard him talking on the phone one morning though. Very low, like he wasn't trying to disturb the other passengers, but I heard him. More like I turned the volume down on my earbuds to listen. I couldn't hear who was on the other end of the phone, but I could hear what he was saying. He told whoever he was talking to that one day they were going to have to try. They were going to have to love them where they were, and only then, when they accepted and acknowledged that they are not perfect and have no room for judgement, *that* is when the right love will find them. He ended the conversation saying, "but until then, you know I'll always love you", then he hung and returned to his daily paper.

He reminded me so much of my grandfather in that sense. He never missed a day with the paper. Sometimes I caught him laughing at the comics, he was so pure. He embodied the joy that I tried so hard to feel alone.

I think one day he saw me crying on the platform before the train came. He never said anything or asked me what was wrong, but I knew he could tell. I saw his eyes through the pieces of hair that tried to hide mine. They looked sorry, as if he was apologizing to me. The next day he gave me a origami heart made out of the comics in his newspaper. I still have it on my dresser at home. It said I hope you have a good day, and if I wasn't already, after that I sure was.

I missed my grandpa. He was so gentle. Nothing like my mom. She has always been so strict, so by the book, so to herself. She never let me in the way she did my grandpa. After he died, she picked up a lot of shifts at work. One time I heard her on the phone telling someone I reminded her too much of him and everytime I smiled it stung like a fresh wound.

My seat began to rumble, aggressively shaking my feet off the seat, bringing my attention off the journal. No one even flinched. Were they feeling the same thing I was? I called out to Mr. Malone. He was staring at me but not answering. The person sitting next to him isn't moving either. It's like they were frozen. Right when I stood up the train came to an immediate stop and threw me across the aisle.

When I woke up, my head felt like a boulder, way too heavy

to be on my shoulders. The train was so dark, I felt around searching for the nearest pole to get my balance. After slowly crawling down the aisle, I found one. It took me a minute. I must've hit my head on something when the train stopped.

Mr. Malone was gone. Everyone was. It was just me.

The train door slid open, no announcement was made, but the stop didn't look familiar. I get out but there's no platform, no parking garage, nothing but grass. The sun beamed in every direction but the heat never touched me. All I felt was breeze, just warm enough to not cause a chill. I walked straight for a while and still nothing but grass. I turned around and the train was gone. There was nothing else for me to do but continue to walk. I began to scream. There had to be someone around.

I saw a shed in the corner of my eye and I began to run. I get there abnormally fast as if I didn't even run. Something was very different, very odd. It was very familiar but unfamiliar at the same time.

I saw a guy exit the door, but he doesn't seem to see me. I followed him for a while and now there is a community in my view. From the shed, it was only the very starched grass, now all of a sudden streets appeared. I keep walking, amazed by it all. Every few feet a new kind of view. He popped up from behind me.

"Are you following me?" the guy from the shed yelled, holding something in his pocket.

I backed away.

"No, I mean yes, I mean I'm lost. I think."

"You *think* you're lost?" he said, slowly lowering whatever was in his pocket

"The train dropped me off in the field back there. You were the first person I saw. So I thought I'd see where you were headed." I said slowly, putting my hands down.

He reached into his bag.

"Yo! What are you doing?" I said, hands returning back to their initial defense.

"Chill, I'm just putting on my mask. I'm assuming you don't have one since you aren't from around here." he said, reaching back into his bag to grab me an extra one.

"A mask? Why do I need a mask?" I said grabbing and inspecting it in my hand before placing it on my face.

"You do know that we are going through a global pandemic,

right? Where exactly are you from?" he said looking at me quizzically.

"Umm, Ohio." I said through the medical mask he gave me.

"Umm, we're in Ohio." he said, still looking at me oddly. "Follow me, I want to show you something."

"I don't even know you," I said, not moving

"You obviously watched me long enough to feel safe enough to follow me," he yells back over his shoulder, still walking.

I jogged to catch up.

"I don't even know your name," I said trying to keep up with him. His walk felt more like a run.

"Oh, you didn't hear that when you were watching me," he said with a low laugh.

"No, smartass I didn't."

"You're a feisty one. I like it."

"And I'd like to know your name," I said getting a bit annoyed

He told me that his name was Jordyn, but his friends called him Jay. He looked like a Jay. Too smart for his friends, but dumb enough to fit in. Confident with a healthy dose of cocky.

This was not the Ohio that I remembered. Everything looked much different. Almost artificial, too good to be true. The grass was too green, the clouds looked like you could reach right up and touch them. No one was out and about like my Ohio. There were no cars either. Maybe that's why everything appeared more vibrant, more lively.

He began to walk back towards the place where I first saw him.

We arrived at the building and he stopped around the corner where I was hiding. He swapped his blue mask for a more fitted black one with gold adjusters near the ears. The door scans his eyes then unlocks. He motions for me to follow him quickly, so I do. We enter, and the space is huge. Nothing like the broken down sheds outward experience. He tells me to be quiet and make sure I'm not seen. So I crept around the corner as he walked to join the crowd.

Everyone is wearing black and white, a cocktail hour of some sort. Horderves circulating around the room with a champagne fountain in continuous flow in the corner. I didn't understand. He came back around the corner to meet me in a pair of pants that appeared to be tailored specifically for him, a linen shirt, and fitted black blazer.

He quickly changed, throwing his jacket back into the pocket of his bookbag. He dragged me out of there before I had a chance to stand up. He begins to run, I could tell something was wrong.

Night caught up to us before he finally stopped to catch his breath. There was something in the air that made me feel invincible. My asthma would never let me be great, but here, it was like it didn't exist.

Through his panting I heard him talking about how we have to go back tomorrow, but I wasn't too sure. We arrived at a lake and he began to walk through the water, like he parted seas, but the water quickly consumed him. I didn't know what to do, I couldn't swim, but I also couldn't let him drown. I scream, quickly realizing there was never anyone around. So I run, the water soaking my sneakers, adding weight to my small frame. I wailed into the water, splashing around hoping to find a limb to latch onto, and I did. Except he's pulling *me* back to the shore—

completely dry. I just watched the water swallow him and him submit just as freely. Just as he was completely dry, now so was I.

Maybe I died when the train crashed. This isn't what I imagined heaven to look like. Maybe an island, never Ohio.

He began to walk and this time I don't follow. There was too much going on that I couldn't explain so I just sat there. Trying to collect myself, trying to suppress the memory of me almost drowning when I was eight.

He pulled me out of the thought when he came to sit in front me. I looked at him for what seemed like forever. He had the kind of eyes that instantly brings you comfort, the type where even on his biggest smiles they're still as big as moons.

"What are you thinking about?" he interrupted my thought

"Your eyes. I mean—," it was too late now. He'd already heard what I said

"That's cool, I was thinking about yours too," he said, pushing my twist from out of my eye.

"What? That does make sense," I said fiddling around with the grass underneath me.

"What doesn't make sense is how we've been together this

long and you still haven't told me your name. So, I've named you Reece."

"Like the candy?" I laughed.

"Yeah, exactly. You skin frames your eyes perfectly, just like chocolate does the peanut butter." he said. I could feel him looking at me.

"You think my eyes look like peanut butter?"

"Yup. Cmon' Reece," he said grabbing his bag.

"My name is Gabby." I said following him again.

"I like Reece better." he said.

I see the shed again and we're about as far as I was when I first saw it, but still no train. At this point, I wouldn't be surprised if it did randomly appear. Nothing was normal there, but I had to figure out how to get home. Or this was home now.

"Jordyn—", I stopped before I finished my statement. I wasn't sure I was ready for this answer.

"Am I dead? Is that why I can't get home?" I asked, slowing down my stride.

"Um, I don't know. Do you feel dead?"

"I feel lost. Nothing feels familiar and I have nowhere to go and it's getting dark."

"I don't know if you're lost, dead, or in the in-between as they say. But it's dark now, so if you want you could stay at my place and I can help you figure it out in the morning."

"I don't know… I don't really know you to be staying at your house." I said, noticing a neighborhood appearing in front of me. It was a huge house, mansion like almost.

"Listen, you have nowhere else to go and I would rather you stay in one of the bedrooms in my house than a bench on the side of the road." He said standing on the stairs of his house.

I'm pretty sure there were at least six bedrooms in this house and I really didn't have anywhere else to go.

"Okay, but don't even think to try anything." I said, meaning every last bit of it.

"Scouts honor," He said holding up three fingers.

"You were a boy scout?," I said rolling my eyes pushing past him

"If you count spending one saturday afternoon in a church basement, then yes I was."

This house felt very familiar. Very clean, but messy enough

to know it was lived in. We seemed to be the only ones in the house. I hear Jay's voice echo through the living room, shouting for me. I followed his voice into a room with periwinkle walls. He told me that I'd be sleeping there. He left to get towels for the bathroom. There was a bathroom in the same room as the bed. Now that, that was heaven. I never had a bathroom in my room. Jay came back with a towel, loofah, and a pair of basketball shorts, and a t-shirt.

"I didn't see you with a bag, so I'm assuming you don't have any clothes." he said.

"Yeah, thanks," I say, taking the pile from his hands and placing it on the bed.

"Alright, I'll let you get settled and cleaned up. Let me know if you need anything."

I didn't even want to look in the mirror to see what I looked like. I definitely didn't want to guess how I smelled, so I just stepped directly into the shower. It felt so good. So warm and inviting. I didn't know where I was going to go. I didn't even know where I was. How did I go from my morning train ride to in the middle of nowhere, which is really Ohio, but there are no buildings until you walk up to them, and there's no people around to ask questions to but Jay, who's name may or may not be Jay, but I'm staying at his house anyway.

It was just so much and I didn't know how to process it all.

If I was dead, did mom know? They would tell her right? They had to. I never leave the house without my wallet, so if I did come up missing they'd know who I was.

I realized I'd been in the shower for a while when I looked down at my pruney fingers. After I got dressed, I ventured out into the kitchen to find Jay sitting at the dining room table. There were two placemats set.

"Hey, I made pasta if that's your thing." he said motioning towards the second bowl on the table.

"You cooked this?" I said sitting down surprised.

"Why are you so surprised? A mans gotta eat."

"Not surprised, impressed." I said through my fork full of food.

Dinner was pleasant. Surprisingly delicious. We were the only people in the house. His parents were doctors so they rented an apartment near the hospital so they wouldn't have to come home during the pandemic. He didn't seem too sad about it though, he's probably been throwing parties or something. Given the opportunity, what kid wouldn't?

Me, this kid wouldn't. My mama didn't play that, and I love my life too much to try.

After dinner we took our bowls in the kitchen and I helped him clean. He washed, I dried, it was a nice little system. I could hear a movie coming from the living room. I couldn't make out what it was though.

"What are you watching?" I asked, putting the last dish away.

"Oh, it's some movie. I just threw it on for noise. You can watch it with me if you want."

We settled into the couch and the movie was keeping my attention, but I noticed I was keeping Jay's.

"What are you looking at?" I laugh, nudging him hard enough to tilt his body.

"Can I ask you something?" he said, turning his body to face me.

"21 questions, GO!" I said, facing him too.

"How old are you?"

"18, 19 in two weeks."

"Favorite color?"

"Olive. Come on, hit me harder."

"Do you believe in love?"

"I'd like to say I do."

"Elaborate."

"I don't think I've ever experienced love. I think I have an idea of what someone feels when they're in love. I don't know. I've never seen a successful relationship, so I don't know exactly what I'm supposed to do or how to navigate it. But short answer, yes I do."

"Are you scared of it?

" I think I'm scared of losing myself *in* it. I see so many of my friends getting hurt by the people they love and I just don't believe that love is supposed to hurt you like that. I don't believe it's supposed to break you down. That's why I'm so focused. I'd never let anyone break my spirit the way I've theirs."

"That's fair. I guess I feel the same way. My parents have been together since before I was born, but I don't think they were ever happy. Or maybe they were, and that's just what marriage does to you. I think one of their mutual friends set them up and everything else was history. I know now they work alot, so if they aren't sleep and on work trips they're bickering about something"

He takes a long pause.

"You seem to carry a lot on your shoulders, and I'm not just talking about that oversized momma bag, but you seem to be in your head a lot. A lot more than a normal person, which is okay because I definitely don't think you're normal, but you don't always have to do that. It's okay to let someone in. I know it may be scary, but we need it. Don't shut everyone out okay? You don't have to be like your friends. Just be you Reece and it'll come naturally."

We talk about a lot. I probably do more of the talking than he does, but he doesn't seem to mind. I don't remember going to sleep, but I did. I woke up to the smell of eggs and warm croissants. I head into the kitchen to a note.

I'll be back. I made you breakfast,

I hope you like egg and cheese croissants.

-Jay

That was so sweet of him, almost as sweet as the croissants. I imagine this is how they taste in France, we talked about that too. He told me he loved it there. He said the first time he went was the first time he felt like himself, like he didn't have to be what someone else wanted him to be. I was too embarrassed to say that the train was my France. As I ate the croissant, it took me back to the rumble of the tracks, pulsing through my body from my seat. Parts of his house smelled like the cologne of the men on the train, musky, manly, and refined. That hour and half on the train was paradise, my freedom from the real world. Those steel doors protected me from the expectations and demands of life. And if I was dead, this couldn't be heaven. My grandpa always said that heaven was personalized just for me. That God paid so much attention and he loved me so much that he'd only give me the best, a paradise, because I'm blessed.

To some, those dirty trains may have been a burden, but if I could take a train everywhere, it'd be my first choice. I really hoped I wasn't dead. I never got to say goodbye, I never got to tell Mr. Hanson thank you for paying attention and never expecting anything in return.

Jay came straight to the kitchen as I took my last bite.

I asked him about the shed, when I saw the blazer hanging out of his bookbag.

"Is that your job or something?" I said, pointing to the bag

"What?" He said looking in the fridge.

"The place inside the shed. Is that your job." I said putting my plate in the sink.

"Um, not exactly. It's more like a—" he trailed off. "Like a club"

"Like a country club?"

Big house, that would make sense.

"No, like a society type club." he said, still turned away from me.

"Secret Society?" I said, intrigued now.

"If I tell you, I'll have to kill you."

"Well we don't know if I'm dead yet, so I take the chance."

He started walking up the stairs passing the room I'd showered in, into a room with lighter walls. It was beautiful, princess like. Canopy bed, matching dresser and vanity, straight from the catalog.

"A 7? You look like you wear a seven." he said coming out the closet.

"In what? Shoes?" I said

"I couldn't tell what size dress you were so I pulled a couple. Pick your favorite, put them in your bag and meet me back downstairs in those clothes in thirty minutes.

I picked a pair of black strappy heels with a black chiffon asymmetrical one shoulder dress. I pinned my hair up in a high bun with a swoop bang. If I had to leave the house, my hair would at least be done.

I met him downstairs, bag on shoulder.

"You ready?" he said, swirling a set of keys around his finger.

I followed him to the garage to see a lineup of cars. He picked the black Nissan. Safe choice. We arrived at the infamous shed. He parked in the back, out of view from everyone else and began to change. He wore a simple black tux this time, still tailor just for him. I followed suit, and took the dress out of the bag. I got in the back seat so he couldn't see me. He knocked on the window before opening the door. I was still strapping my heel. He just stood there.

"Speechless? That's a first." I said reaching out my hand to him.

We walked to the door where it scanned him like before. We stopped just as we got in.

"Here put this on." He said, handing me a black mask that matched his.

He linked his arm with mine and we entered the space. It was much bigger than what I'd seen before. Same vibe, more people. I instantly felt out of place. He whispered into my ear how nice I looked. It eased my nerves a little bit, but not completely. I probably should've picked one of the other dresses. These women looked incredible. We both grabbed drinks from the servers. Flutes with just enough to take the edge off.

The night progressed and it turned into a big networking fest with music masking the conversations.

I spoke with a woman, about my writing. She told me that she owned a magazine and would love to set up a meeting with me. Her assistant couldn't have been much older than me, her youthful skin mirrored my own, but if she was anything like the women in this, I'm pretty sure she could afford top of the line skincare.

I wondered what connected everyone in that room. What was the point of them meeting? Jay went off on his own, he told me he had business to handle. I didn't know what kind, I probably should have asked more questions like that last night.

I had been on my own for a while by the time everything was coming to an end. I walked back towards the bar to get a better view of the crowd. Jay was nowhere to be found. I was an outsider, I didn't need to draw too much attention to myself. I kept my head down, and my hands close. As I hurried across the room to a corner I overheard two servers talking about how it was about to come down, and how all the spoiled brats were going to get what they deserved. I didn't know what they meant by that, but I knew I had to find Jay before I found out. I moved briskly through the crowd running into one of the servers. Silverware and glasses fly everywhere. The room began to spin around me. The voices became inaudible, and everything went black.

***

"Miss? Miss?" a man tapping me on my shoulder said.

I looked around confused as to where I am

"Yes? Where am I? Who are you?" I said clenching my bag.

"I'm the conductor. I think you may have fallen asleep and missed your stop. You're free to ride it back around, I just wanted to make sure you were okay?" he said, looking at me confused.

"Umm, where's your mask?" I asked

"Mask? For what?" he asked, stepping back.

"The pandemic? Aren't we in a global pandemic?"

"Ma'am? Are you sure you don't need me to call anyone?"

"What? Um, no I'm fine. Thanks for letting me know." I said trying to collect myself.

I take my headphones off trying to focus on what was around me. Trying to bring myself back to reality, I reach into my pocket for my phone, but it's not there. Something fell onto the floor. I reached down to pick it up and it's a heart. Much like the one Mr. Hanson gave me.

Only this one said,

Until next time Reece

-Jay

***

The next day on the train I see Mr. Hanson. He smiles and says hello. I want to leave it at that, but I have to ask him if he remembers.

"Mr. Hanson?"

He looks up from his paper.

"Could I ask you a question?"

He nods.

"Yesterday? What do you remember from the ride?"

"Well, we go on, somebody's baby just wouldn't stop crying, and I supposed that was it. Nothing out of the ordinary. Same ole, same ole. Why do you ask?"

"No reason," I stopped. I was sure there was a crash. "Can I ask you one more question?"

"Shoot." he said.

"What's your first name?" I instantly get nervous.

"Jordyn, but my buddies call me Jay."

SHAKIRA WASHINGTON

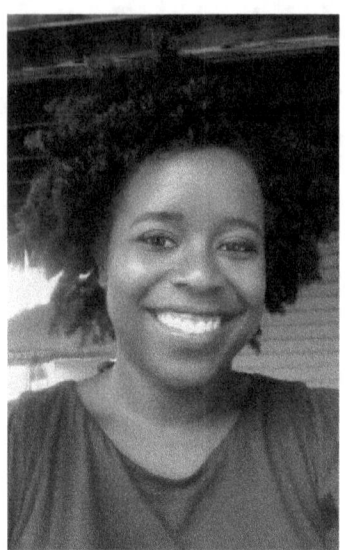

Hi, My name is Shakira Washington, and I am a proud millennial. It sounds like a contradiction, but it's not an insult or a nickname that describes an entitled lazy, often offended generation. To me, its badge of honor. They told Millenials to follow a set of rules to be successful, and we followed those rules but, then the world change ((9/11, Wars, Great Recession of 08, 2016 Election, and COVID-19 all by 30!). Instead of being praised for being adaptable, they criticized us for not staying on course.

We created our path and carved out our own space within society. It may have been unconventional, but what's the point of being young if you don't challenge the status quo.

My experiences as a millennial and as a Black woman has inspired my writing. I feel passionate about sharing my point of view and ultimately showing that black women are multidimensional relatable, sometimes even ordinary human beings. We are magical, yes, but we lead healthy lives and have everyday problems just like everyone else. The more spaces we occupy, the more our presence as black women becomes normalized. One thing I learned as a black woman and as a millennial, is that no one is going to speak for you or invite you in the room or give you a seat. If you are not your biggest cheerleader, your biggest advocate, then who will be? So be loud, be honest, and make them uncomfortable!

The Last Intern

Chapter 1

A year ago, before the pandemic, Natasha Worthington, or Tasha as her friends call her, wore chiffon blouses and hip-hugging pencil skirts that showed off her athletic but beautiful legs in a sophisticated way. She pranced into high rise buildings, with her designer stilettos hitting the tile floors, as she was on her way to meet her interior design clients. Tasha's life in New York City was full of style, taste, and expensive furniture.

Tasha prided herself on her appearance, her tight dense curls, always looked moisturized and healthy. She rarely straightened her hair, for she created a variety of updo styles with her natural hair, that eluded professionalism and made people feel at ease, especially in majority-white spaces. Despite her talent and experience, many years pass before her company promoted her to senior designer. Being the only black woman in her firm, Tasha expected to work harder to get ahead. However, it was still painful to hear every time she did not get promoted. She knew that she could not let them make any more excuses for passing on her, which is why she invested so much into her appearance. Tasha splurged on salon hair care products, designer shoes, clothes, and bags and even made her Harlem apartment look like a catalog. She was taken more seriously and, therefore, finally promoted just before the quarantine began. However, she did have the chance to collect one check on that generous bump in pay, so she was left with her debt from her expensive shopping ventures.

Like many industries, the interior design industry suffered during the quarantine of 2020, especially the area of private clients that her firm specialized in. Suddenly, people's priorities shifted, and they no longer needed decorative vases or a tufted velvet chaise. Her clients, who were typically very wealthy, held on their purses and retreated to the Catskills or the Hamptons when the virus ravaged New York City. In March, the interior design firm furloughed her and Tasha collected unemployment and lived off her savings. Like many people, she believed the quarantine would only be a few weeks, and she would soon be back to work, however weeks turned into months, and eventually, she was out of work for almost the entire year. Not listening to advice from her friends, Tasha continued to spend money on designer goods, instead of saving money until going back to work. The pandemic and quarantine lasted longer than she expected, and the firm did not rehire her. Tasha eventually used all of her money, ran up her credit card debt, and could not afford her designer clothes and loft apartment anymore.

It was embarrassing, to say the least, especially since Tasha liked being independent. But on a cloudy fall afternoon, through prideful tears, Tasha called her best friend Christina, or Tina for short, and begged to sleep in the spare room in her in tiny Newark, New Jersey apartment. Tina had previously offered to let Tasha quarantine with her earlier that year. Still, since Tasha is boastful, which often came off as arrogant, she told Tina she had everything under control and not to worry.

Tina, who has been friends with Tasha since college, knew it was not true, but Tasha always made up her mind without assistance. Tasha answered Tina's ad looking for a roommate near Drexel University in Philadelphia, and the rest is history. Tina agreed to let her move on that fall day, of course, and Tasha was humbled and grateful that she did not have to move back to her parent's row home in Philadelphia.

Tasha sold most of her lavish home décor and designer clothes on secondhand websites, which surprisingly were still pretty lucrative despite the economy. Pieces of her ripped away every time she made a sale. A little bit of sadness mixed with relief. On the one hand, she was able to use the earnings to pay down her credit card debt. However, Tasha built a versatile and expensive collection, and she tied her identity into her new polished look. Without the fancy clothes, catalog apartment, and professional makeup, who was she?

When she arrived in Newark, Tina picked her up from the train station. She looked like a European backpacker combined with New York Hobo chic. Tina had never seen Tasha so un-put together. Her afro was in a messy puff, and her usual glowing, vibrant brown skin looked dull and tired. She was drowning in these dusty denim overalls, and oversized backpack, and beat up old sneakers. Bags hanged from every limb, and she was dragging a large rolling suitcase behind her. She was only able to bring clothes, mostly jeans, t-shirts, sweats and undergarments, a few pairs of shoes – gym sneakers, a causal canvas slide, combat boots, and gladiator sandals. Most essential, she packed a suitcase filled with hair and hygiene products. She donated items not sold to a local women's shelter—her last act before leaving Harlem.

Tina tried to play it cool and walked up to Tasha and gave her an awkward side air hug around all of her bags.

"Hey, girl!" Tina exclaimed, trying to put some positivity in this situation.

"Hey, Tina," Tasha replied flatly, feeling defeated and tired.

"Alright, I parked in a bus zone, so let's move quickly."

Tina grabbed a few bags, and they briskly walked to her jeep. They piled her stuff in trunk and backseat.

"How are classes? I bet it is annoying to be still taking online classes." Tasha said as they drove down Raymond Blvd to Tina's Ironbound apartment.

"I decided not to return to Princeton this fall."

Tasha's eyes widen, and she shot over a surprised look. "Christina Daniels!"

"Wait, let me explain. I love studying Psychology, and I have been putting off getting my masters, but this summer made me realize why I was so reluctant to go back to school in the first place." Tina explained, and Tasha just gave a resounding "un hun."

Tina was the opposite of Tasha in every way. Maybe that was why they became fast friends in college. Tina's demeanor is more relaxed and weighed every decision under logical and emotional consideration. Unlike Tasha, she could be hot-headed and impulsive. Tasha knew that Tina had given this some serious thought.

"So, what are you going to do? Continue working at the nursing home?"

"Well, I quit the nursing home a few weeks ago. It was exhausting. Business picked up during the quarantine, and I had to work there like three days in a row, with very little sleep, to adhere to strict social distancing guidelines. I burnt out." Tina said, keeping her eyes straight ahead.

Tasha nodded sympathetically. Once college courses moved to strictly online, Tina started working more hours at the nursing home since she did not need to commute to Princeton twice a week. Her job was deemed essential, so she has not had a break all summer. Unlike Tasha, who spent the summer alone destroying her credit score, Tina was risking her life during the pandemic to help others. Tasha felt guilty and very selfish.

"I just need a break. I need to get away from all this. I want to help people with their mental health issues, but I can't do that until I deal with mine." Tina said as if she had rehearsed this line and recited it many times.

"I completely understand. We can be unemployed and do some soul searching together." Tasha replied jokingly.

"Well, that's what I wanted actually to talk about," Tina shouted back toward Tasha at the bottom of her steps as she struggled to open the front door with bags in her hands.

They stumbled into Tina's apartment, and Tasha immediately tripped over boxes. Looking around confused, Tasha's large brown eyes widen even further, a look Tina knew was the precursor to Tasha losing her temper. She quickly grabbed the bags from

Tasha's hands and put them in the spare room. Tasha sat down at the café style kitchen table covered with stacks of psychology books. Tina locked the door behind them and ran over to the fridge and poured two glasses of rose.

"Breathe, Tasha," Tina said calmly. "Breathe."

"What's going on? Why are there boxes everywhere? Are you going somewhere?" Tasha asked, discombobulated.

" Breathe," Tina demonstrated." "Have you been doing yoga, like I told you? It's great exercise and will help relieve all that built up stress."

"Don't patronize me. Just tell me the truth." Tasha took in another deep breath and let out a long sigh. Then she took a long sip of wine.

"Okay," Tina said in her signature, sing-songy voice. "I'm moving to Colorado to work on a cannabis farm. I will learn about the cultivation of different marijuana strains and their properties. I will learn about alternative forms of healing and find a more holistic approach to helping people. White male academia only works for white male academia. Black people have different traumas that need a different approach. There has to be better ways to connect, to heal, to deal with trauma, and I want to learn about them."

Tasha let out a loud hysterical cry, and Tina consoled her.

"It's going to be ok. We can still have Rose Fridays. We will just have to do it virtually. And you're going to be ok. You're the smartest, bravest person I know. I love you."

"I love you, too," Tasha replied in between sobs. She was not sure if she was crying because her best friend was moving across the country or that she sold all her worldly possessions and had no idea what she was going to do for money, but the combination of all those things came crashing down at this moment.

"Sometimes, you just need a good cry," Tina whispered. Pulling away and looking into Tasha's brown eyes. "When is the last time you had a good cry anyway?"

Tasha wiped away her tears and grabbed a tissue before responding. "Beyoncé's Formation tour, when she covered that Prince song."

Tina threw her head back and laughed, "Wasn't that like five years ago?"

"Yeah. Yeah, it was."

Chapter 2

Tasha rushes into her apartment and hastily changes out of her paint-splattered denim overalls and into her navy-blue cleaning uniform and white apron. As of late, Tasha's outfits consist of shapeless overalls that make her look like a middle schooler, and an unflattering cleaning uniform accompanies a headscarf that makes her look like a grandma. Five days a week, she rushes from her day job as a painter and tiler for a contracting company and to her evening job as a cleaner at a high-rise office building on the upper west side of New York City. It may seem crazy to commute into the city just clean a building, but COVID-19 Sanitation is a booming business right now and pays well. Everyone is very cautious of the disease coming back, so more affluent neighborhoods invest in completely disinfecting buildings. Instead of spending days in luxurious high rise apartments and her evenings socializing with cocktails at happy hour, Tasha now fills her post-pandemic life with paint, dust, and ammonia.

Tasha slicks her hair back into a disheveled bun and wraps a headscarf around her head with a messy bow at the back. She runs down the stairs from the second-floor apartment she is subletting from Tina and catches the bus into the city. Tasha prefers to take the bus in the evenings. It's the end of rush-hour, and the long bus ride allows her to sit down, be off her feet and relax, even if it is just for an hour. She usually puts on a podcast if she is more awake, but if she feels sleepy and wants to take a quick nap, she listens to a meditation playlist that Tina made. According to Tina, they slow rhythms of the music sync up perfectly with relaxed breathing. Tasha thinks it is a bit over the top, but she admits that she gets in a perfectly rejuvenating 45-minute nap. Tina always gives the best advice, and she truly does miss her best friend.

One year ago, she lost her career, and six months ago, her best friend moved away, and she feels stuck in this small apartment all by herself. And in two months, she turns 29 years old. The late twenties are supposed to be the best years of her life, but maybe her 30's will be better.

The bus pulls into Port Authority bus station, and Tasha squeezes out of the bus with the other passengers. She adjusts her mask as she hurries down the aisle. Public transportation still requires people to wear masks as a precaution, and they do not even allow passengers to step on the bus or train without one. Usually, the shame from the New York Public, with everyone staring at someone holding up the line, is enough for people to comply with the mask mandate.

Tasha walks along 9th avenue. She could take the subway, but she prefers the exercise and to breathe in the air without a mask. Her stomach growls, and she figures that chicken Caesar salad wrap she ate around 3 pm is not enough to sustain her for the rest of the evening. She spots Magnolia Bakery and wanders in. At this time of night, the bakery is mostly empty, and there are limited selections left. However, Tasha proclaims to love all sweets equally, despite contributing to her quarantine weight gain last year, she loves cupcakes the most. She grabs a German Chocolate cupcake and messily eats the whole thing before making her way out the door.

She enters the office building through the back entrance. The security guards check all the cleaners temperatures before entering the building. Sanitation cleaning is taken very seriously, in that if buildings can afford it and not all buildings can. Tasha swishes mouthwash in the bathroom and grabs any personal items to place in her apron, since once the suit is on, Tasha cannot remove the suit until the end of her shift. Yes, this does include bathroom breaks. She learns from a veteran coworker the faster you clean, the sooner you can pee, and they still have to pay you for the entire three-hour shift! Tasha dresses in the secure backroom and clocks in at precisely at 8 pm.

This particular office building has 12 floors and with one cleaner on each floor. Tasha makes her way to the 9th-floor offices of Lakes, Rivers, and Waters, which she thinks is a funny name, or that they are trying to be ironic. She has an efficient system and cuts almost 30 minutes off her cleaning time so she can leave work a little early. She always starts her cleaning routine in the kitchen. Everyone thinks that bathrooms are the worse because of what goes on in bathrooms, but you can splash bleach and disinfectant everywhere and clean in one quick swoop. However, with kitchens, their dirty dishes and forgotten moldy lunches in the fridge, and she cannot just go splashing chemicals where people eat. Some of the worse smells come from rotten food. People are disgusting in kitchens. They never heard of rinsing off a plate? Stuck on food is the worse! The amount of wealth and prestige doesn't make a difference. All people are equally untidy in kitchens. They scatter the dishes around the sink, but not in the sink. a Tasha rolls her eyes as she sees the mess. She then works her way to cleaning out the fridge. If she does not wipe it down daily, it will start to smell.

While the dishes are soaking, she wipes down the counters and tables in the kitchen. The offices of Lakes, Rivers, and Waters are quite spacious, and the kitchen is straight out a designer showroom. Tasha admires the black speckled granite counters, the off white porcelain tile floor, and the stainless steel appliances. She is not sure why this office needs a gourmet kitchen, but she guesses if they can afford it, why not have it. While walking back toward the kitchen sink to start washing the mound of dishes, Tasha glances at the bulletin board. Usually, she doesn't pay attention to flyers on the bulletin board, but then she sees big black block letters on fluorescent pink paper. She only notices it because of its lack of design sensibility. She takes another look at the pink flyer and reads:

"INTERNS WANTED FOR SUMMER 2021 POSITIONS FOR FINANCE, MARKETING, AND GRAPHIC DESIGN. MUST BE A COLLEGE STUDENT OR RECENT GRADUATE."

"Hmm, I bet I could do this," Tasha says out loud while her hands are elbow deep in suds. Tasha dries her hands and carefully tears the name, email, and phone number information from the bottom of the flyer and unzips her suit a little bit to place the slip of paper in her apron pocket. This difficult to do with two pairs of gloves on, and especially since she is not supposed to unzip the suit under any circumstances, but she figures this is important and lets it slide.

The next day while at her day job working for the Cousins Contracting Services, Tasha is arranging a kitchen backsplash tile in a chevron pattern and contemplating what her next steps in life are. Something she has plenty of time to do while doing repetitive tasks. By the time she leaves her cleaning job at 11 pm, takes the bus home, and jumps in the shower, it is well after 1 am. Tasha passes out and has to promptly wake up at 5:30 to be at the back at her day job by 7 am. Initially, the Cousins do not want to hire Tasha to do contracting work since she is overqualified. A constant problem, too much experience to be an assistant, not enough to be a leader, and they, do not want to hire anyone with a college degree. They pay employees to work, not to think, at least that what they keep telling her. She hides her degree on her resume, at least that how she keeps the cleaning job. She tries restaurants, hotels, gas stations, grocery stores, before seeing a social media posts about the opening at the contracting company. Tasha resorts to begging, and the Cousins finally hire her. The Cousins compromise on her rate, and once she showcases her design skills, and advises some kitchen and bathroom design tricks, the Brother's business started to boom. She quickly became an essential part of the team, earning the title "Lead Designer." However, this is not a glamourous position, because the group is so small, everyone pitches in for tasks around a new property.

Tasha enjoys this work because it allows her to be creative. However, tiling and painting all day are physically demanding, so Tina suggests doing Yoga three times a week to help alleviate some of her muscle stiffness and improve her overall mental health. So, on days when she leaves the construction sites at early, she squeezes in an hour an online yoga class, before eating a quick dinner and catching the bus into the city to clean offices.

The routine is becoming exhausting, and Tasha knows she cannot keep going at this pace for long. Over the past ten months, she lives humbly and tries to save every penny. Budgeting is not one of Tasha's strong suits, but she manages to follow a strict weekly allowance that leaves some extra funds to put into a savings account. In a couple of months, she will have enough saved to maybe take a break, while she starts to look for interior design work again. Lost in her thoughts, she barely hears the call to end for the day.

"Tasha, Tasha? That's a good stopping point. We see the pattern, and the weekend crew can finish it." One of the senior contractors says.

Tasha nods and put back her assigned tools, before making her rounds telling everyone to have a good weekend. One of the exterior painters jokes how she looked like a little kid in her paint-splattered overalls and slicked back afro puffs. Everyone laughs in unison, but it gives Tasha an idea.

Chapter 3

Rose Fridays with Tina turns into Rose late Saturday afternoons since Tasha gets home late and sleeps away most of her Saturday. They have a standing appointment every Saturday at 3 pm. The two-hour time difference makes it lunchtime for Tina and a late brunch for Tasha, but she doesn't mind rose for breakfast. Tasha rolls out of bed and logs into her laptop just in time for Tina's face to pop up on the screen.

"Heeeeeyyyyyyyyyyyyy!!!!!!" This exaggerated "Hey" kind of makes fun of the stoner stereotype that people typically expect when Tina tells them she works on a marijuana farm.

"Hey, girl," Tasha says between yawns and runs to in kitchen to grab an apple, a wine glass, and an unopened bottle of rose.

"So, this week, we are working a strain that will help deal with PTSD. Think hallucinogens without the hallucinating part. We want the patient to relax and open their subconscious mind." Tina says as she adjusts her bright pink hair wrap covering her coils. Tina's intense brown skin pops against the vibrant color.

"That's awesome. I think I have some PTSD. Maybe that will help me unpack it all." Usually, Tina does not like it when Tasha made jokes about mental health issues, but today she can tell her tone is a bit different.

"Everything ok, Tasha?" Tina says cautiously, lowering her glasses and staring directly in the camera, pausing, and waiting for an answer before taking a bite of her vegan egg sandwich.

"I have this idea. You're going to tell me I'm crazy, and I do not think this through. I'm just becoming discontent, and I'm tired. I mean, I'm grateful for the Cousins for giving me a job, and I'm grateful I have food, an apartment, and money to pay my bills. But I didn't get this degree and work this hard just to settle because a global pandemic is ruining my career trajectory!"

Tina tries to quietly chew her sandwich, knowing it is rare for Tasha to express her emotions. She is hot-headed, impulsive, and her feelings usually come out at the most inopportune times. Like in college, they are grocery shopping, and the store does not have flaming hot chips, and Tasha snaps at the poor stock boy. It is not about the chips, of course; it is about a lousy critique she from her professor on her project. They do not buy any groceries, but they go next door to the liquor store and buy cheap wine and drink it out of paper bags as they walk back to campus.

"Ok, so..." Tina replies gently, trying not to force the conversation.

"I just feel so stuck. And I know I don't have a fall back plan, and I am terrible at saving money, but I don't think I can settle with being unhappy. I'm a hard worker. They say be smart, work hard, go to college, be professional, be successful. When did they tell us how to survive a recession, and a pandemic, and the Black Lives Matter Movement? Not to mention, we need to close the gender and racial pay gap, and build generational wealth, and stop workplace harassment, eat a balanced diet, have a skincare routine, exercise daily, get eight hours of sleep and embrace your blackness and make time for self-care! I can't do it all. I'm only one person. I follow the rules, kind of, I play the game and look where I am? Cleaning the offices of former legacy students and the grandsons of white men who work hard once."

"Breathe, Tasha. Breathe." Tina whispers.

"I don't mean to job shame. Being a cleaner is a very noble and tough profession. I just want five minutes to feel sorry for myself. I don't want to be the strong black woman right now. I need a break. I need something to go my way for once."

They both sat silently, staring a each other through computer screens. Tina takes a slow sip of her wine, while Tasha takes a long gulp and slams her glass down to refill, before speaking.

"I don't want to complain. I know a lot of families are still struggling, especially since there is not any more government aid. I have to do something different, and I need to take a risk. I feel stagnant, and it's time to be uncomfortable."

"Well, Tasha, taking risks is not your problem. It's thinking things through before acting or speaking."

"Thanks for reminding me, Tina. I have a plan this time. I

promise." Tasha says confidently.

"Do I want to know this plan?" Tina asks suspiciously.

"No, the less you know, the better."

Chapter 4

"A Flyer, really Corey? Why did you let me go through with this? Malcolm says in an aggravated tone.

When Malcolm initially propose d the idea of summer interns as a way to bring in diversity and a fresh perspective to the offices, he envisions going posting on college or recruiting or job boards.

"Sorry, Mal, you know my father can be a little, um, what's the word?"

"A Boomer!" Malcolm shouts. "No one advertises on flyers anymore. It's the 21st century!"

"Hey, you can't say the B-word around here! You know that." Corey replies, trying to soothe Malcolm. They are longtime friends since business school, and in the past decade, Corey only sees Malcolm get angry during the NBA playoffs. However, he is not sure of the reason for upset today. Malcolm is usually reserved in the office and rarely shows emotions.

"We still have fax machines!" Malcolm shouts again.

"Alright, Mal, let's go talk and walk and grab a coffee."

They exit the building on 9th avenue and walk towards Central Park.

'What's going on with you today, Mal?

Corey stops walking and lays a hand on Malcolm's shoulder. Despite both being former college athletes, Corey is a few inches taller with long, lean limbs that tower over Malcolm's six-foot well-built frame. Malcolm, determine to walk off his anger, finally stops and sees Corey standing still, his sandy blonde hair blows gently in the wind.

"Why are you standing there like a Calvin Klein model?" Malcolm irritatingly asks.

"Oh, really, you think I'm good looking enough to be a model?" Corey retorts. "You know you could model watches. All you have to do is hold your hand to your face, and they will zoom in on the watch and those beautiful green eyes."

"Shut it." Malcolm snaps, and they both stare at each other before bursting out laughing in unison.

"I'm sorry, man. I didn't mean to get upset. It's just I got my job at LRW because of an internship. This place gives me a network and connections, and I just want to give the same for some kid out there."

"But my father is stuck in the past." Interjects Corey Waters, son of Charles Waters, one of the current senior partners, and grandson of one of the founding members of Lakes, Rivers, and Waters Consulting, a marketing and advertising agency. Corey often anecdotes that his grandfather and the founders are the original MadMen.

"Well, you said that, not me."

"You called him a boomer, Mal," Corey replies amusingly.

"Well, if he is going to suggest posting a flyer in the kitchen of the office building that we work in, to attract top college talent, then he deserves the label of boomer, in the negative sense. They want us to find ways to bring in youth and diversity, and we are advertising to old white men."

Malcolm finishes his rant and sits on a nearby park bench, and Corey sits down beside him.

"Hey, we're both going to be old white men soon." Corey jokes. "Look, I know you're feeling the pressure because my father is retiring, and a senior partner position is opening up, and you want it. Hell, you deserve it. But even if my father decides to keep it in the family, there are rumors Rivers is retiring soon also. So, there might be two senior partnerships opening up."

"Doesn't Rivers have a nephew graduating soon?"

"Yeah, from high school, it will be another decade or so before he is eligible to be a partner. And who's to say the kid wants to be a consultant. He may want to be a doctor or an artist or something."

"Did you have any choice on your path?' Malcolm asks.

"Well, no, I wanted to a pro basketball player, but that is a kid dream. Anyway, let's get back. We have a meeting soon. And the internship program will be great. Trust me." Corey reassures Malcolm, and they head back to the office.

Corey succeeds at cheering Malcolm up and can put a smile on anyone's face. Malcolm is the serious, studious numbers guy, and Corey is the charismatic, life of the party and can make the most stupid thing, marketable. Their tag-teaming efforts make LRW a considerable success, at least before the quarantine. However, they lost many of their clients, and some did not recover after the pandemic was over. Currently, LRW is looking for a boost. However, the resurfacing of Corey in blackface at a college frat party hurts the agency's image. Modern businesses want to work with agencies that reflect the diversity of their customer base. They also have difficultly retaining employees because the partners still favor Malcolm and Corey, and it is difficult for new consultants to gain clients. Although they have been vocal about this, the partners rarely change their minds. So as of right now, it's just the two of them, their secretary Hilda and the three senior partners who are close to retirement and only come in the office periodically.

Malcolm walks back to his desk and logs on to his computer. An email from a name he doesn't recognize pops up.

Natasha Worthy

Subject: Graphic Design Internship

To whom it may concern,

My name is Natasha Worthy, and I am a recent graduate of Drexel University. I am applying for the Graphic Design Internship. Please see my resume attached and link to my portfolio below.

I look forward to discussing future opportunities with you.

Thank you,

Natasha Worthy

Malcolm clicks on the link to her website and is thoroughly impressed. He claps his hand together and says to himself. "I think I found my first intern."

Chapter 5

"Hello, Natasha? Can you hear me? Malcolm echoes on the old dusty computer in one of the conference rooms. He jots a note to get <u>NEW</u> computers before the interns arrive because this is embarrassing. How have they pulled million-dollar accounts still using Windows 95?

"Yes, Mr. Banks, I can hear you and see you." Tasha replies in her "white voice" that Tina teases whenever she raises her voice like five octaves and wears a forced but professional smile.

"Please, please call me Malcolm."

Tasha set up her virtual interview space in the corner of the living in front of a bookcase. She decorated with old vases and books she got from the thrift store – and she only spent $20! Companies conduct most interviews are virtually now. An in-person interview is a guaranteed hire, so it is scarce to get one. Since the team is so small and they are looking to rebrand, the internship will be in office, but if they hire full time, they have options to work remotely.

Tasha's first interview with Malcolm goes swimmingly

well, and Malcolm requests that she speaks with some of the senior partners and show them her impressive portfolio. Tasha is initially flattered to meet the partners, but, as the weeks drag on and she keeps receiving apologetic emails from Malcolm about the availability of the partners and delays. She is starting to get paranoid. Maybe they are doing a background check? Perhaps they are verifying her references? Tasha is very careful when she creates this new persona of Natasha Worthy, a recent college graduate from Philadelphia, PA. It is true she graduated from Drexel University but seven years ago, not last month, and it is true she is from Pennsylvania. Tasha holds an interior design degree, not a graphic design degree, but she is proficient in all the latest technology and has a keen designer eye. She uses her interior design portfolio website as a template and temporarily unpublishes it from online. She even googles herself and to make sure there are no surprises. Luckily, with the new Marvel film releasing this summer, if you google Natasha Worthy, there are about 500 hundred pages about Black Widow. Social media is a bit tricky. For that, she enlists the help of an old college pal with freakish computer skills and never asks too many questions. To transform her Instagram into that of a typical 22-year-old college student instead of a professional woman approaching 30. Thank goodness no one remembers myspace, and she deletes her Facebook after the 2016 election.

Tasha reinvents herself into this young bright eye, ready to take on the world 22-year-old instead of a burnt-out millennial at her wit's end. For the summer, she is no longer Tasha Worthington, Interior Designer, but Natasha – which is her real first name, but she hates it –Worthy, Recent Graduate, and Graphic Designer.

"Yes, Malcolm. I can hear you."

"Great, let's begin. So, the first person you will speak to is Bob Lakes, his background is in economics so his questions might get a bit technical, but you are smart, so do your best. Secondly is John Rivers, he's more a marketing guy and tends to be a bit wordy, but nod and ask one good question. Lastly, you will speak to Charles Waters. The firm is his family's legacy, so he has more of a stake, so just show him your enthusiasm and passion. You're going to do great. Um, Good luck!"

Malcolm kicks himself for that awkward ending, and why does he get the feeling he is more nervous than she is. Everyone knows she is the best candidate, so why are they stalling and making Natasha jump through all these hoops? Is this because he vouches for her? Is this some sort of test from the partners? It makes him uneasy, and he hopes they see that Natasha is a good fit and that he has an eye for talent.

Tasha senses that Malcolm is nervous for her to speak with a few old white men. However, her work as an interior designer for New York's elite puts her into many rooms where she is the only black woman or person of color in general. The industry is not known for its diversity. She often works with disgruntled husbands who believe she is convincing their wives they need a $10,000 sofa. The wives never needed convincing and were always too happy to spend their husband's money. She knows how to prove herself over and over again, especially since most people do not think you need a degree for her line of work. Despite her track record, every new client tests her knowledge and skills. It also does not help that she was just a designer, not a senior designer, even though she handles clients by herself without supervision. Her promotion is long overdue, but it is a game she has to play as a black woman.

The interviews go as expected, with a few unnecessary comments on how young she looks, and one of the partners opens with a "Hey girl." Otherwise, she is poised, professional, and throws in a few overly exaggerated laughs at the punchlines that are not necessarily funny. Overall, Tasha feels she made a good impression. The internship is a risk, and this entire scheme could backfire. She is not one to lie; in fact, she is usually too quick and brutal with the truth. There is a pit of guilt she feels for going through this whole process, but she knows this is the only way to get out of her rut. She acts as a desperate woman.

She frantically checks her email every day until she finally receives one the Friday before Memorial Day Weekend.

Hi Natasha, thank you for being patient, and I would like to say, congratulations, Lakes, Rivers and Waters Consulting selects you as a Summer 2021 Intern

Our secretary, Hilda, will be sending over formal documents and information you need to know. Still, I want to personally let you know and not keep you in suspense over the holiday weekend.

Enjoy your holiday weekend, and we will see you Monday, June 14th.

Sincerely,

Malcolm Banks

Tasha squeals on the bus ride back to her apartment, but then a sense of dread overcame her. Two weeks! Her current day to night look consists of dirty overalls and bleach laden scrubs. She still has a few blouses that she kept for virtual interviews, but as for a pull together look to work in an expensive office on the upper west side, well, that's going to take some effort. She decides to skip her Friday online yoga class and head to the thrift store before her cleaning shift.

Chapter 6

The first day of a new job is always stressful, but the circumstances are different this time. Not only does Tasha need to pretend she is 22 years old and a graduate, but she needs to fit in with Gen Z. Unlike Millennials, Gen Z has a swagger and confidence. People criticize Millenials for every decision they make that does not align with the traditional set of goals in the "American Dream." Media blames them for ruing everything from the chain restaurants to disrupting the diamond industry. There is not time to buy diamonds when you are working three jobs to pay off student loans. Millennials have a morbid sense of self, almost self-deprecating. Still, although everyone from family members to the media thinking Millennials are lazy and entitled, they did not give in to the criticism and redefine what success and happiness are in the 21st century is.

Tasha is typically one of the younger employees in the interior design firms. They give her more work, not only because she is a black woman, but because they believe she is not working as hard as her older counterparts. A co-worker makes a shady comment about how he has to do mathematics on paper in school, not a fancy calculator or smartphone, and that is why Millennials are not money savvy or good with numbers. Tasha snaps back and yells, "OK, Boomer, what math do you use to tank the economy?" Everyone in the room gasps, but Tasha refuses to apologize.

Tasha's mind is racing as she jumps on the train early to make sure she is not late on her first day. She arrives 45 minutes early and sits on a bench in Central Park, sipping her latte before walking over to Lakes, Rivers, and Waters. She takes a deep breath and recites her greeting over and over again.

"Hi, I'm Natasha, recent graduate of Drexel in Philly, Graphic Design I'm currently staying in Newark at a friend's place while she is away on an Internship out west." If she repeats it enough, then hopefully it cements in hear mind and comes out as the truth. She smooths the wrinkles on her skirt and looks down at her feet. Luckily, she keeps at least one pair of designer Tory Burch flats, just in case. They are her first purchase from moving to NYC six years ago. At the Thrift store, she finds vintage, yet subtle pencil skirts in black, navy, tan, and gray patterns and stripes and pairs them with her nice blouses. In her mind, she can pull off a retro meets modern twists to the business professional dress code. Keeping her face fresh, she only applies tinted moisturizer - shade medium deep - eyeliner, mascara, and nude lip gloss. She slicks her hair back into a twisted updo and accessorizes with a headband. Tasha, who regularly uses contacts, decides to wear her thick tortoise plastic-framed glasses to pull together her look. The glasses also make her look younger. On the outside, she looks presentable, but on the inside, she feels more like the generic version of Blair Waldorf.

Walking in Lakes, Rivers, and Waters as an intern and not the cleaning lady is nerve-wracking. Tasha has to continually remind herself to pretend like she has never been here before. It feels surreal, and she tries to keep her composure because if it is one thing she learned about wealthy people during her time in NYC, is that they can smell the middle class, and they can sense fear. Tasha walks into a conference room with a small sign on the door that reads, "Welcome Summer 2021 Interns." An older woman is laying out platters of breakfast, Danishes, quiches, and donuts. Tasha has not seen this much food on one table in so long. Her stomach grumbles, and her eyes widen, and she whispers, "Sorry," as the Secretary turns around and looks at her with a warm smile.

"I'm Hilda, dear, and you must be Natasha."

Tasha is not sure how she is supposed to take that comment but generously waves since not everyone feels comfortable shaking hands post-pandemic.

"Yes, I'm Natasha. Nice to meet you, Hilda. Um, how did you know it's me?"

"Well, I recognize your voice, and the way Malcolm describes you is very accurate. He says you have the most beautiful big brown eyes. But you didn't hear that from me, dear."

Tasha blushes and is feeling fluster when another intern walks into the room. She turns around and sees a petite girl with auburn hair cut into a blunt bob. She thinks to herself, "Is that how young I used to look?" Suddenly she is second-guessing her decisions to do this internship, and worse, she is lying to her parents and Tina. They think she is freelancing a couple of days a week. Graphic Design is still a creative field, and she has the skills to be successful. Technology is not slowing down anytime soon, but the need for redecorate summer homes fluctuates. This internship is a chance to improve her current situation and set herself up for a better future. She just has to keep reminding herself that.

"Hi y'all, I'm Jolene. I'm the economics intern from Vanderbilt in Tennessee." A sweet soft southern voice says, and Tasha introduces herself as well.

"Natasha, from Drexel in Philadelphia, for graphic design." She waves back, and they exchange polite conversation about books. Tasha can already tell she will get along swimmingly with Jolene and that immediately puts her at ease.

Last to enter the room are three men, all standing over six feet tall. Tasha recognizes Malcolm from her interviews and assumes the cocky young one is another intern but does not know who the tall blonde one. She is suspicious immediately. Are they having an 8 am boys club meeting? Tasha forces a smile on her face as the men introduce themselves.

"I'm Malcolm. It's nice to meet you, Natasha, finally." Malcolm sticks out his hand, and Tasha hesitates for a moment and reaches out for the handshake. His handshake is firm, and she matches the intensity of his grip while staring intensely into his green eyes. It is almost as if he is trying to send her a coded message. The handshake only lasts a few seconds, but it feels like time stands still.

The next person to shake her hand is Corey Waters. She puts two and two together, and if she squints, she can see in 30 years he will become Charles Waters. Corey is friendly but looks right through her. He is a man that commands respect when he walks into the room and never has to return that respect.

The last intern is Spencer Taylor-Brown, the marketing intern from Columbia. From the moment he walks into the room, there is a growing tension between him and Tasha. He looks Tasha up and down when and Tasha knows he spotted her thrift stores skirts immediately. With a coy smile, he reaches his hand out, and Tasha goes to meet his grasp, but he pulls back and jokes, "Oh, sorry, I don't want to get whatever parts of the virus are still lurking in Jersey. You understand, right. I'm Spencer. You're Natasha, right?." He leans in so only she can hear, "The diversity hire."

They all take a seat, and Tasha looks around – She is the only 'one' in the room.

Chapter 7

Throughout the summer, the interns work together to improve the LRW website and mobile app to make it more interactive and user friendly. Immediately Tasha and Spencer argue over every concept from user experience technology to the font style. Jolene tries to keep the peace between them.

"Let's use Times New Roman. It's professional and academic." Spencer retorts as he throws his hands up before taking another bite of his everything bagel.

"No. Helvetica, it's modern and timeless. And Sans serif fonts transfer better from desktop to tablet to mobile." Tasha replies and takes a sip of her chai latte.

"What? San-serif? Don't be snobby, Natasha!"

"What did you just say? Am I snobby for having an opinion?"

"You have an opinion on everything. You're so..." Spencer trails off as Malcolm and Corey enter the room.

Everyone stops frozen and turns to look at them. Tasha and Spencer stand toe to toe as Jolene outstretches her arms to create space between them. They quickly jump back and awkwardly take their seats. Malcolm senses the tension in the room, but Corey sits and grabs a bagel.

"Hey guys, we just want to check in to see how the project is going. Can you believe we're already halfway through the internship? Anyway, we want to view the run-through of your presentation. This way, we can provide any feedback or answer any questions."

"Ok, I'll start," Jolene says assertively, as Spencer and Tasha look at each other in embarrassment.

Jolene gives an overview of the improvement of the app and the financial impact of making such changes. She stands at just under five feet tall and has a sweet, soft southern accent. Jolene always looks polished, a true southern belle, but she dislikes that title. However, Southern women are some of the strongest, smartest people she knows, it can have negative conations, too, especially in the North. People think she is simple, and always joke "Jolene, like the song," and they start singing off-key. To end the horrendous singing, she usually recants how her mother was listening to Dolly Parton when she went into labor and gave birth to her kitchen. Born six weeks premature, which is what her family attributes her small frame too. She is the youngest of five siblings and has four older brothers. Her family is very protective of her, especially since Jolene continues to struggle with childhood illness into adulthood. Due to her diseases, she spends most of her time taking online classes. Vanderbilt is her first time in a formal educational setting and being away from home, although it is not far from her family's Belle Meade estate. However, once the pandemic begins, she transfers back to online courses. Jolene's two years at college convinces her family, she is independent enough to do a summer internship. Although she wants to apply and interview like anyone else, her father, who runs his share of successful businesses, calls up an old friend. Initially, she is displeased, but if this is the opportunity to be independent, she cannot be too picky. This internship is her chance to be a grown woman or as much as a 21-year-old can be. Jolene tries to exude confidence; she knows she is smart and good with numbers, but she is more reserve and tends to get lost in the crowd. This internship is her chance to stand out.

"Perfect, Jolene. Excellent financials. Who's next?" Corey asks, and Tasha and Spencer both jump up at the same time, but Spencer grabs the laser pointer before Tasha can reach it. Damn short arms.

"I'm next," Spencer says boastfully and clicks to his slides. He always gets his way, and Natasha is messing with his chances of landing a job here. Corey has put in a good word for he attends Corey's Ivy League undergrad alma mater. What's her deal, anyway, he thinks? What does she have to prove? Maybe he is overcompensating a bit. His older sister is about to graduate from medical school, and his younger sister is about to graduate high school at fourteen. Maybe it is middle child syndrome, Spencer coasts through life because of his family name, good looks, and wit. His father is always scolding him on work ethic and being humble, but that is not his style. Spencer knows he does not have any other redeeming qualities, so he goes with what works.

"Great, Spencer," Corey responds. "And I love the use of the font and graphics."

"Thanks," Spencer replies. "I want to Helvetica because it's modern, and it is easy to read on desktop and mobile websites."

'Great Idea!" Corey says as he gleefully claps his hands.

"Hey, that is my idea, and I create all the graphics." Tasha grunts and rolls her eyes at Spencer.

Before Spencer responds, Corey interrupts. "Well, Natasha, it's a team effort, and you have to learn to be a team player here at LRW. Right, Malcolm?"

"Yes, Natasha. We see the hard work all of you are putting in. It is a team effort." Malcolm agrees.

Tasha wants to snap back, but then sees the look in Malcolm's eyes and shuts her mouth. Spencer gives her a smug look of satisfaction while Jolene gives her a sympathetic nod and mouths, "I'm sorry."

"Well, thank you, everyone, and I'll send my notes to you later," Malcolm states and walks abruptly out of the room.

Typically, Corey is more nonchalant and goes with the flow and lets Malcolm handle all the grunt work and details. It is a combination that works well for them. However, he notices that

Corey is particularly interested in this internship. When Malcolm first introduces the concept, Corey is not enthusiastic about it all, saying, "He doesn't want to be a babysitter for the summer." Now, he dives in headfirst and acts like a true leader. However, Malcolm is still disappointed that the interns are not well, more diverse. Jolene is the daughter of an old family friend of Rivers, and Spencer is a legacy student from whose parents are former clients, now retired. Neither of these two candidates need this internship as a stepping stone. Malcolm stakes his reputation on Natasha's performance this summer. Maybe talking to her in private will help. But is that suspicious? He does not want it to appear he is playing favorites, but perhaps he is too hard on her. The way her big brown eyes look at him whenever he supports Corey and not her is gut retching. He needs to find a way to be more supportive of Natasha. Never one to make rash decisions, Malcolm decides to think about how to handle the situation over the weekend.

After the meeting, Tasha is visibly upset, not one who can hide her emotions in her facial expressions. Jolene walks over to her in an attempt to comfort her.

"How are you doing, Natasha?"

"Oh, hey, Jolene, good job in there. And sorry about Spencer and me. I'll try to keep my cool. It's not fair that you are stuck in the middle."

"It's ok I have four older brothers. They wrestle and throw things. You guys are easy compared to them."

"That explains why you're so patient. I'm an only child, my parents had me in their forties, so I didn't grow up watching cartoons, but the Diagnosis Murder and Price is Right." Tasha states, hoping it sounds more sarcastic than pathetic.

"Oh, really, no siblings? Somedays, I hope. And everyone loves Price is Right. It's an American treasure." They both laugh, and Jolene hesitates. "I am wondering if you will like to come over this weekend. We can have a sleepover. I'm staying in my father's penthouse on the upper east side, and we have plenty of room and food, and..." She trails off. What is she thinking? Do people call them sleepovers in your twenties? She is new to this, making a friend's business. Homeschooling does not prepare for these types of situations.

Tasha laughs, "Sure, that sounds like fun. Um, I have plans tonight, but I can't come over tomorrow night. Say around 6 pm? Text me your address. Can I bring anything?"

Jolene squeals and Spencer looks up from his desk suspiciously. They laugh, and Jolene says in a whisper. "Yes, 6 pm sounds great."

"

Chapter 8

"Hey girl, we have to keep Rose Brunch Saturday to a crisp 2 hours. I have plans tonight."

"Ohhhh, with a man?" Tina exclaims.

"No, one of the inter-freelancers invites me over a girl's night. We're going order Thai food and watch the reboot of Gossip Girl." Tasha almost slips there. The ruse she tells Tina and her parents is that she has a freelance graphic job at an ad agency in the city. She tries to keep details to a minimum, so she does not get caught up in her lies.

"Oh ok, well, that's nice you are making friends, honey," Tina replies in a motherly tone. "I am worried you are going to spend the rest of your life in those ratty denim overalls."

"They're not ratty, and they are my work overalls. It's what I'm supposed to work in!" Tasha responds defensively.

"All I'm saying they are becoming a crutch. The Tasha I know doesn't settle. So, it's nice to see you out there retaking risks."

"I thought everyone hates when I take risks?"

"Well, yes, we do, but it always seems to work out in the

end. It's hard to keep up with your train of thought, but after a while, your unpredictability becomes predictable, and it's comforting that you are living your life that way again."

"Well, hopefully, this risk works out, or I'll be back to kitchen backsplashes, or worse."

"Why, is something wrong at the freelance job?" Her psychology degree enhances Tina's skills with reading between the lines.

"You can tell something wrong because I did I three-second sigh instead of two?" Tasha jokes before continually. "There's this trust fund baby. He is working my last nerve, and of course, we are working on a group project together with Jolene, the other intern who I'm having dinner with tonight. They will hire one of us full time at the end of the summer, potentially all three of us, if we wow them, but he is standing in my way. He takes credit for my idea in front of our supervisors! So, I call him out on it, and they tell me I need to be a team player."

"And the hot one with the green eyes and the mysterious past? Tina asks, hoping to hear more about this supervisor Tasha describes as the hot one with something to hide.

"He agrees with them. I think he is on my side, but he always proves me wrong." Tasha says, feeling deflated.

Tina takes a sip of her rose. "I mean, they kind of have a point. You don't work well in teams. You're an only child, and your parents are older, so you like alone time. It's not your fault. It's just your nature and something to work on." Tina says gently, knowing what Tasha reaction is going to be.

"What? Tina, you're playing therapist now? I'm a team player. I just hate when people steal my ideas and get credit for them."

"Is this your first day being a black woman?" Tina asks, and they both sit in silence, sipping their rose. "You have to kill them with kindness, wait for the right moment, and when you get your opportunity to shine. GLOW!"

"To that, I'll say cheers!" And they imaginary clink wine glasses through the computer screen.

Tasha arrives at Jolene's penthouse promptly at 6 pm. She does not want to seem rude, and she is excited to see the inside of the apartment. She searches online the building on the way over, and the photos are spectacular, she expects nothing less from Jolene's apartment.

Jolene opened the door wearing magenta silk pajamas and her beautiful auburn usually pristine with perfect straight bob, is naturally wavy and thrown into a messy ponytail. She greets Tasha with a hug then offers her a glass a champagne Tasha takes her shoes off by the door. She decides to wear high waisted black leggings and a cropped band t-shirt with sneakers, hoping for an edgy vibe since silk pajamas are not part of her wardrobe. As she expects, the penthouse is immaculate with all the latest design trends. The foyer is a beautiful mosaic tile before transitioning to cherry wood floors throughout. The entrance leads to a living room, dining room, and a sitting room, which is just a smaller living room, usually without a TV, used for more formal guests. They walk past a wet bar and buffet in the dining room, as Jolene continues to give Tasha a tour. An older woman dressed in a black pantsuit intercepts them before they walk into the kitchen.

"Ms. Claiborne, your medicine is on the kitchen counter, and please don't overdo it on the sweets."

"Yes, Mrs. Johnson. Have a lovely evening," Jolene responds, feeling embarrassed, and Mrs. Johnson exits through the front door.

"Sorry, I let my staff have the weekend off, so we can relax, but Mrs. Johnson insists on checking in on me. I had a series of childhood illnesses, some that still bothers me." Jolene explains.

"No worries, but sweets?"

"Oh, that's what she called alcohol. It was a code name for

it when I was younger. I thought it was a dessert for my parents. Anyway, I can handle champagne and wine, but beyond that, I'm still testing it out."

"Well, that's ok, I love champagne and liquor can be overrated."

Jolene laughs and leads Tasha into the kitchen. "This is my favorite room in the house," Jolene exclaims, and Tasha is in awe. "When my family remodeled a couple of years ago, I told them I wanted the kitchen to be fun, to feel like Tennessee. Every other room is so serious and so modern. I love it!"

Tasha looks around, eyes wide and mouth agape. The walls are bright yellow with off white traditional cabinets, beautiful Carrara marble countertops, and tiled marble floors. The hardware is copper with a hammered copper farmhouse sink. Tasha walks to the center island that is surrounded by eight barstools and is the same size as her entire apartment.

"I've worked on some gourmet kitchens, some country kitchens, some farmhouse kitchens, but this takes the cake."

"You worked on kitchens?" Jolene asks, looking confused.

"Um yeah, summer job back home. I worked for a contracting company, and I did tile work. Kitchens and bathrooms." Tasha catches this mistake and remembers she cannot let her guard down too much.

"That must have been hard work?"

"Well, yeah, it's backbreaking, um, it was backbreaking, yeah." Tasha stumbles. "Sorry, I think I need to drink some water, the heat on the subway, you know."

"Oh yes, so sorry, I've been rude." Jolene scrambles off the barstools and climbs up a step ladder and opens the distressed white traditional style cabinets and grabs a glass. She places the glass on the marble countertops.

"Do you want sparkling, tap, or bottled water?"

"Sparkling. No ice, please."

"Oh, stop now, you don't have to be so formal. We're not at work. I know the guys are hard on you, especially Malcolm." Jolene pours the sparkling water in the glass and passes it to Tasha. She takes a long gulp before responding.

"Well, I think he means well. I spoke to him a lot during the interview process, but I don't talk to him at the office, but he does send me lots of emails, usually with comments or feedback. Though he sent me a curt email yesterday, so I imagine I will get a talking to on Monday."

"He treats you like a child, and I wish I were brave to stand up to Spencer like you did. He can be a real ass sometimes!" Jolene covers her mouth and then lets out a little giggle.

"Jolene Claiborne!" Tasha says in a pretend southern accent. "Well, he is not all bad. I don't exactly make it easy for him, either. I mean, I fight him every step of the way. Maybe I should let him win a few arguments now and then."

"And inflate his ego even more? That's a dangerous game."

"Or it could have the opposite effect. Maybe we will find some common ground. Malcolm is right, though, I shouldn't let him get under my skin." Tasha admits and finishes her glass of sparkling water before returning to sipping champagne.

"When did Malcolm say that?"

"Oh, in his email yesterday. He says, and I quote 'Natasha, you have potential, but you need to check your ego and don't let Spencer's ego get the best of you. We'll talk next week." Tasha mocks in a stern baritone voice.

"Hmm," is Jolene's only response.

"What, Jolene? Spit it out." Tasha says as she pours the champagne bottle to refill her glass. "Oh shoot, we're empty."

"That's ok. We have more, trust me." Jolene opens an unsuspecting closet door, which is actually and beer and wine fridge.

"My parents like to party," Jolene says, quickly changing the subject.

A couple of bottles of champagne later and the girls are in the living room dancing to Drake. She drinks out of the champagne bottle, knowing she is going to regret all of this later. Jolene is standing on a chair, making impressions of Malcolm, Spencer, and Corey."

"I'm Corey, and I work for my Daddy! I'm Malcolm, and I'm mad and mysterious. I'm Spencer. I overcompensate my insecurities with arrogance!"

Tasha is lying on a heap of oversized decorative pillows they arrange on the floor, holding her sides from laughing.

"I didn't forget, Jolene. What were you going to say earlier?" Tasha can hear her words starting to slur.

"I was going to say…I think…, Malcolm likes you. Like, likes you, likes you. Like a man likes a woman!" She squeals, and Tasha remembers how young Jolene is in comparison to her.

"Oh, no. I don't know."

"I know he's like 35 or like 40, but he is unmarried, and I don't think he has any secret kids."

"Corey has secret kids." Tasha jokes. "But he is not that much older than me. Just a few years."

"Natasha, like ten plus years!" Jolene replies and begins to open another bottle.

"No, no Jolene, water. I'm not as young as I used to be." Tasha says as she begins to snuggle in between two body-sized pillows.

Jolene stops opening the bottle and is a bit lost with Natasha's last couple of statements. She thinks maybe she likes older men and she is very mature for her, so in her mind, she is older? Anyway, Jolene forgets about all this and continues to have tonight.

Chapter 9

It's Wednesday morning, and Tasha still feels like she has a hangover from last Saturday night. Getting drunk at 29 is not the same as getting drunk at 21. Plus, the night gets hazy after they leave Jolene's kitchen, and but she does not remember saying anything stupid, so hopefully, it is true. She receives a ping from her email and sees it is a message from Malcolm that reads, "Now a good time to talk?" She takes a deep breath and responds. "Yes, coming to your office now."

Tasha stands outside Malcolm's office for a few minutes before entering. He gestures for her to take a seat while he finishes typing. She tries to be calm but then notices a button on her blouse has come loose. She frantically buttons it before he looks up.

"I wanted to talk about your behavior last week. I expect more from you, Natasha." Malcolm says, sounding like a High School Principal. "A lot is riding on this internship, not just for you, but also for me. I want you here, and my reputation is on the line. They are happy to fill your seat as a favor to one of their buddies. I know you can do great things." He is searching for the right words, and he does not want to say it because he does not want to be that guy, but it's better if it comes from him and not one of the partners.

"You need to work on your attitude. There have been complaints that you are difficult to work with, and I frankly don't believe that's true. However, that's the conversation happening. I know you have good ideas, and you're smart, but other people are smart and have ideas, too. You tend to be too outspoken and step on other peoples, toes. I understand the position you are in. I, too, feel like an outsider, like I don't belong here, that I have to pretend to fit in. I'm not saying you should lie, but just be mindful of how you present yourself." He usually is unphased by these critical conversations, but he can see this has hit a nerve. Tasha shifts in her seat and clears her throat. He waits for her to say something, but she just stares at him, statue-like. "We want this to be a place of collaboration and teamwork, and we all have to make compromises." Malcolm finishes; this is not his best work. He is off his game.

Tasha looks up at Malcolm, every word stings, and he reminds her, as many have done before, that she is a guest in this position of privilege, not a permanent resident. At any moment, they can take this opportunity away from her without remorse or compassion. Outspoken is a soft way to say "too loud," and they use that word to try to silence intelligent black women; it is a term that is very familiar. Difficult to work with is code for "she questions and challenges their ideas," without just conceding because they are ivy league educated white men, so they must be correct or smarter than her. She meets this type of opposition often, and she handles it in stride. However, she did not expect this type of misogynistic old boy speech from Malcolm. She is beginning to think he is not on her side after all.

Malcolm lets out his breath and looks directly in Tasha's big brown eyes. "Natasha?"

"Yes, sorry, sir. I will take your words under advisement and will do better going forward. I promise I will not disappoint." Tasha looks up, and her eyes meet his. She tries not to show emotion, but if she stays in his office any longer, she will burst into tears. "Are we done, sir?"

"Yes, but Natasha," before he can finish, she flies out of his office, grabs her purse, and jumps in the elevator to exit the building.

Jolene sees Natasha sprint out of the office and head toward the door.

"What was that all about?" Spencer asks annoyingly.

"I think Natasha is upset."

"She's always upset about something. She is never happy."

"That's not true." Jolene snaps back. "I'm going to see what's wrong with her." She grabs her purse and walks behind Spencer's desk.

"Go, then. Bye." Spencer snarkily remarks.

"You're coming, too," Jolene commands

"No, why, but." Spencer rises to leave, but before he can protest, Jolene grips his arm and swings it around his back, putting in him in an uncomfortable hold.

She whispers in his ear, "I have four brothers. I know things. Let's go." Although she is the youngest of five and too small to play with her brothers, she pays attention to how her mother commands the room when she walks in and tries to imitate that. Her mother can keep up with her active linebacker sized brothers, despite her being only an inch taller than Jolene.

Jolene and Spencer walk to the park and finds Natasha a sitting on a bench. They both stop before she sees them.

"Now, Spencer, go over there and make amends. This is your fault, so fix it."

"How is it my fault?" Spencer asks, genuinely confused.

"I'm tired of playing peacemaker, and Natasha admits that she is tired of fighting with you, too. So, I think if you talk it out, then we can move forward and focus on our presentation, which is only a few weeks away." Jolene says, hoping she sounds confident and not nervous. This can end in disaster. It is very unpredictable, which version of Natasha and Spencer steps into the ring each day.

Spencer humbles himself and walks over to Tasha. "Hey, Natasha, can I sit? Jolene, well, she not as sweet as we think. She twisted my arm to get here. So here I am."

"Are you here to gloat? I'm sure you heard I got scolded." Tasha snaps. Spencer throws up his hands and starts to walk away. "Wait, Spencer, that's childish. I'm sorry. Please take a seat." She gestures to the space on the bench beside her. Spencer starts to walk back to her, and then an older woman sits down on the bench, leaving just enough space in between. Spencer begrudgingly squeezes in the center seat. There is a long awkward pause before they start speaking.

"I'm sorry." They both say in unison and then start to laugh.

"You go first, Natasha."

"Ok, well, Spencer, I'm sorry I fight with you over everything. I feel bad because I write you off, but you have good ideas, and I'm learning that we have more in common than I originally thought."

"I'm sorry, too." Spencer begins. "You know I don't say that often. Most people let me do what I want and go along with what I say. You are the only person who challenges me, besides my dad, of course. I look forward to our daily disagreements, and I admire your passion, Natasha. You play the game like you have nothing to lose."

"I have a lot to lose actually, so I'm terrified," Tasha whispers.

The older woman at the end of the bench offers them candy, and they politely take it.

"I've said some pretty mean things about you, and it was all out of frustration. None of it was true." Spencer adds.

"Well, tell that to Malcolm, or your buddy Corey. The frustrating thing is Spencer, is after this internship you are still going to have plenty of options. One way or another, you're going to be ok. I don't have a backup plan. If I fail, it's back home to rural PA. So, I would just appreciate it if you use your privilege to help me, not hinder me."

"This isn't easy for me, either Natasha. My father expects me to fail. I always scheme my way in and out things. And you're right, there will still be options, but that's my problem. I know there are other options, so I never try. I want to try, and I want to make my father proud. I'm not trying to make excuses; I'm just trying." Spencer's voice breaks a little the end of the statement and hunches over, placing his hands in his face. "Look, I'm a spoiled little brat and a trust fund baby, and all those other things, but I'm going to try to do better, and I will do whatever I can to help you, even past this internship."

"I appreciate you saying that, Spencer. I will try to be more compassionate and a team player." Tasha replies and awkwardly pats him on the back.

"But don't get soft on me, Natasha. I need you to check my ego still, and I'll check you when you too, um, passionate. Deal." He extends his hand, and she shakes it.

"Deal."

The next couple weeks of the internship go pretty smoothly for Tasha, and she is finding her stride between days as an intern at LRW and nights as its sanitation cleaner. Her relationship with Spencer improves, although they still bicker but in friendly spats and not heated arguments. Her weekend routine consists of meeting Tina for Rose Saturday Virtual Brunch and then going to Jolene's for dinner on Saturday nights, so she is not in that big penthouse alone. However, Tasha does not mind the endless amount of food and champagne. For the most part, she avoids Malcolm, and he only speaks to her through email and the occasional hello in the kitchen. Things are starting to look up for Tasha.

Their presentation is approaching fast, but in between practicing and finessing their project, they still need to complete projects for the partners and supervisors. Tasha receives another email from Malcolm, and she reads with his voice in her head. "Natasha, please stop by my office when you have a chance." She is regretting going by Natasha, every time someone says it, she feels like she is in trouble with her parents. She knows enough when her boss says, when you have a chance, they mean -now. It's 4:15, and she hopes she can leave right a 5 pm today.

"Hi, Mr. Banks, you want to see me?" Tasha knows Malcolm hates the name Mr. Banks, but with his attitude the past couple of weeks, he deserves it.

"Yes, Natasha. I hate to ask you this. And I'm sorry for what I said a few weeks ago. I was trying to give you, um, constructive criticism, but I'm afraid it came off as"

"Misogynistic," Tasha blurts out. Then she covers her mouth with her hand in shock that she let her thoughts come out.

Malcolm smiles and nods, "Well yes, misogynistic and a bit racist, so to that I apologize. I hope you can forgive me and we can move forward. I notice you are avoiding me. I do not want our working relationship to be awkward."

"A bit, yes," Tasha whispers. Maybe Malcolm is more woke than she has initially thought. "Apology accepted. Thank you for acknowledging all that, and I will try to do better as well."

"Well good, I hear you and Spencer made amends. That is very mature of you."

Mature, that's funny. Well, Tasha is almost 30, and she does not have time for petty mind games. She does not say that, of course, but she realizes at 21, she would never give in to Spencer, let alone be friends with him. I guess this is what people call growth.

"Thank you," are the only words Tasha can manage.

"Well, good," Malcolm states. Natasha stares at her shoes while Malcolm stares at her, hoping her gaze will meet his, but no such luck, so he proceeds. "You know that company you did those amazing graphics for earlier this week, well they are going to be in town this weekend, so we need to prepare our pitch now. I hope you don't mind if it is not too much of a bother to work a little late today? I know it's Friday, and if we work together, we can be out by 7- 7:30 pm latest."

Tasha blushes at Malcolm's mention of her "amazing work," and she can not be sure, but she thinks this is the Malcolm Banks version of groveling. I "Sure, Malcolm, I can stay. What do you need me to do?"

Malcolm's heart jumps because he expects her to say no, and he feels this a great opportunity to get to know her a little better. Corey makes a good point that he can not be an effective leader if he does not even speak to his employees.

"So, Natasha, I need to print, then hole punch and place presentation slides in a binder." She squeals, and he replies, "I know, I know a waste of paper, but with some of these companies, its baby steps into the future."

"That's so shocking to me. It's 2021, I assume everyone is moving forward, but some of us are just stuck, I guess." Tasha responds, and Malcolm catches that there is a double meaning to her statement.

"Stuck, how?" Malcolm asks, realizing this is his first normal conversation with Natasha.

Tasha takes a long sigh and waits for the printer to keep warming up. "You know, work hard, go to college, try to find a job, pandemic, start over."

"Oh, you had a job last summer that fell through? Now they're saying you need experience to get hired into entry-level positions."

"Exactly."

"Yeah, I graduated in 2007, I started working the day after graduation, but my job laid me off at the end of 2008, right before Christmas. I remember showing up at my parent's house a week early. I didn't tell them until the following spring. I just said they gave me an extra week of vacation since I've been working so hard. I didn't want to ruin the holidays for them and my little brother and sister." Malcolm confesses.

"Wow, it must be nice to grow up with siblings. I'm an only

child, which my best friend says is obvious."

"Obvious, how so?"

"Well, my parents had me in their early forties. They tried for years for children, and they explored every avenue, fostering, adopting, IVF, but nothing panned out. Then one day, my mom went to her yearly OB/GYN check-up, and when she was leaving, the receptionist said, 'Oh, we advise pregnant women to come every two weeks.' My mom is like I'm not pregnant and stormed back into the doctor's office and said, why didn't you tell me and the doctor shouted back why didn't you tell me? There was a standoff in the doctor's office. They had to call my father to get her. She was too distracted to drive. Looking back, she said the doctor was asking strange questions and kept mentioning weeks." Tasha laughs and can't believe she is so open with Malcolm, who for the past few weeks, she did her best to avoid.

"That's an amazing story. I'm sure your parents are very proud of you."

"Thank you." Tasha replies humbly. "um, you mentioned your siblings were young when you graduated college, so not truly like growing up with siblings, I guess."

"Well, yes and no. I'm a big brother, and they treat me as such, I don't try to be a parent. I was an only child for 15 years, so, yeah, it was a bit of an adjustment, but my mom had me young, and my father died when I was a kid, so that was hard." Malcolm gets lost in his thoughts as he reflects on his complicated childhood. He starts to adrift, before quickly wrapping up the subject. Anyway, she remarried, and my stepdad is incredible, and they had twins, that it." Malcolm never spends this much time talking about his family, hoping he did not reveal too much, but it's easy to talk to her.

"So, your dad, if you don't mind me asking?" Her phone rang, and her alarm was going off. It was her 7:30 pm alarm. "It's 7:30 pm, so I should get going."

"Yes, you're right. I'll pack these up and finish the binders at home this weekend. Thank you, this is a big help. And we should leave before the cleaners get here, one of them yelled at me when I was working late a few months back. She kicked me out. I barely had time to save my work." Malcolm says awkwardly and wondering why he is so chatty today.

"Well, good luck with your presentation. And it was nice talking with you." Tasha smiles, and she feels flush all over. Why did she say that last part?

Malcolm boxes up the completed binders and places the remaining piles on top before closing with a lid. He exits the building at the rear entrance that leads to a parking garage. He no longer takes the subway, since he often has to take work home. Driving is more convenient to lug confidential files, especially coming from Long Island City in Queens. It cut his commute in half, especially since he leaves in the morning before rush hour and usually doesn't get home until late.

Tasha usually has time to squeeze an outdoor gym class in Central Park, since indoor gym workouts still make her nervous. Or she grabs something to eat, and she sits in the café the reading or watching Netflix before walking back to the office building of LRW. There is no time for either today. She quickly changes in the bathroom before exiting the building. Tasha grabs a granola bar out her bag and eats it before getting in line to have her temperature scanned.

Malcolm is loading the box into his car, where he sees a line of cleaners getting their temperature scanned before entering the building. He spots, no, it can't be, but he swears, "Is that Natasha?" He shakes the thought from his mind, but then he turns around again and recognizes her big brown eyes peeking out of her mask before she enters through the maintenance entrance. He locks his car door and checks his watch. It's 7:55 pm, maybe the security guard will still let him back in. He runs to the front of the building frantically, telling the security guard he left his phone at his desk, and he will be back quickly. Before the security guard can speak, he swipes his badge and runs into the elevator. Malcolm is not one to make quick decisions, so he is unsure why he decides to sprint back into the building and do what? Confront Natasha? It's not illegal to have a second job, and she is very prideful; it is going to crush her to know that he knows she cleans toilets. He changes his mind, but the elevator pings, and he is at the office doors. He swipes his badge and decides to wait in his office while he figures out what to do.

The day turns out to be a very stressful Friday. Usually, she likes to get here around 7 pm because she knows everyone leaves the office promptly by 5 pm. That way, she can go early and catch the 11:15 pm bus instead of the 12:15 am. She hurriedly puts on her hazard suit, gloves, masks, and makes her way to the 9th floor.

Malcolm hears the doors open to the office open, and he thinks this must be it. It's just a hunch that Natasha cleans this floor. He did not post the internship on any job boards, and she told him a neighbor cleans here and saw the ad. Malcolm did not think much of it, and he is not going to speak to the senior partners that her references include the cleaners. He hopes she sees the light on in his office and approaches, but after a few minutes, he grows impatient and leaves his office to go to the kitchen, where he can hear her doing the dishes.

Tasha scrubs the dirty dishes to the rhythm of OutKast's International Player's Ball. She is rapping along to Andre's 3000 verse. Although there are a hundred ways she prefers to spend her evenings, at least this job does not have any interaction with people, and she can be alone with her thoughts. She turns around, and before she can let a scream, Malcolm puts a hand on her mouth over her mask.

"It's me, Natasha. It's Malcolm." He can tell it is her because of those are the same brown eyes full of anger from weeks ago. He sees the shock, horror, and disappointment in them, and he feels awful. This is a terrible idea, and he doesn't know why he is identifying himself when he isn't in full Haz-Mat gear.

"What are you doing here? You can't be here! Security will freak out! I will get in trouble. I need this job. Just go, just go!"

"Natasha, I just want to let you it is ok. You can talk to me. You can tell me anything. I just want to say." He trails off, and he sees tears start to well up in her eyes.

"Just go, please. And take the back stairs to the rear entrance. Security will penalize you extra money if they see you here."

Tasha stands there frozen, dressed in full sanitation gear, with soap suds dripping from her rubber gloves. He opens his mouth to speak, but she holds up a hand to his face, flicking soapy water on his shirt. Malcolm backs aways and taking a cue from the fury in her eyes.

Malcolm follows her advice and immediately exits, leaving through back stairs that lead back to the parking garage. He sits in the car. "Ugh, idiot. Why did you do that?" He yells at himself.

Tasha is flustered and does a half-ass job of cleaning the dishes, but honestly, she does not know how six people make so many dishes. After finishing her shift, Tasha exits through the back parking lot of the building and sees Malcolm standing by his black Audi. She tries to ignore him and proceeds to walk, but he calls out her name, and she is too tired to make a scene in front of her boss. Tasha walks toward Malcolm and looks at him before opening the passenger side door and sitting down.

"You can drive me down to Penn Station. I usually take the bus because I do not have enough time to take the train.

Malcolm pulls out the parking lot and proceeds to drive. He looks over at Natasha and tries to find the right words.

"Um, I'm sorry. I didn't mean to be invasive."

"Or Creepy?" Tasha replies quizzically.

"Or creepy. Yeah, I don't know what I was thinking. I

thought it was a good idea. I'm not impulsive. It's just ever since meeting you. I feel like there's more to you."

"I can say the same thing about you." There is an awkward pause before Tasha adds. "Like Corey is an open book, well he never stops talking. We don't know much about you. Today is the first time you mention your family. We speculate you are a government spy."

"I'm not a government spy, trust me. I'm just a private person."

"Ok, I can respect that."

Sensing the conversation is becoming stale and is making Natasha uncomfortable. Malcolm begins to elaborate to ease the tension.

"I met Corey when I was in grad school. I went back to school to get my MBA after I lost my job during the '08 recession. I thought it would help me get my foot in the door somewhere, which it did, but it also put me in more debt." He takes a deep sigh. "Anyway, I needed an apartment because my lease was up, and Corey was looking for a roommate. We had some classes together, and we've been friends ever since. He got me the internship at LRW, and they hired me. I've been there ever since. That was ten years ago."

"That's not a juicy secret. You know someone who helped you get somewhere. That's networking. Not a big deal."

"I'm not finished yet. Look, I know you think I'm harder on you than the other interns, and that's because I am. I know how they think, I hear how they talk. They are old school. They aren't going just to give you a job because you're a hard worker, talented, or deserve it. They are…"

"Racists? Is that why you pretend to be white, or at least not part black?" Tasha says, then immediately slaps a hand over her mouth. She lacks a filter at this time of night. Her eyes widen, and she tries not to look over at Malcolm as she can feel his glare on her.

"How did you know?" Malcolm replies calmly and is relatively relieved that someone one knows.

"We know our own. Plus, a couple of weeks ago, you were behind on your hair cuts. I know why you keep it short. Once you get some length, I can see some texture."

"My hair gave it away?" Malcolm asks, confused.

"Well, that and you treat me differently than the interns. At first, I thought it is because I am black, but then I realized it is because you are black and you are trying to protect me. Also, something you about being an outsider: I figure you were trying to relate, but it stuck with me. Plus, you are buddy-buddy with Corey and the partners."

"The partners like me because I make them lots of money and Corey likes me because I do all the work and it makes him look good. I am his permanent wingman."

"Oh, I see," Tasha replies sympathetically.

Malcolm takes a deep breath. He has never told anyone of this story. It is just a narrative that plays in his head so he could justify his actions.

"My father is black. He and my mother were separated, but he lived down the street from us, so I saw him every day after school. He retired from the army due to health issues. I was 10 when he died. He had a hard outer shell, but I loved him. He taught me respect and discipline." Malcolm pauses. "After my father died, we moved back east near my mother's family. She eventually met my stepdad, who is white, and they married. She is a Banks, and my twin siblings are Banks, so I am a Banks now. I was born Malcolm Johnson. I was about to start high school, and everyone assumed I was white, and I just never corrected them. People treated me differently when I was with my stepdad than with my father. I can't even describe it. It's unreal."

"I can't even imagine. Just existing, you know, not having to explain yourself all the time or prove why you have the right to exist," Tasha says through tired yawns. "But how does your family feel about this?" She wonders.

"Well, my Stepdad legally adopted me, so it's nice to feel apart of the family. When I was in high school, we went on a father-son camping trip with some of my classmates. My stepdad overheard the other parents talking about how they didn't invite the black boys in my class on the trip because they were "too urban" and didn't know how to camp. I went to a mostly white private school, so there weren't too many black kids. My stepdad didn't say anything, but on the way home, he straight up asked me, "Did you ever tell your friends about your father?" I didn't say anything, and that was my answer. He brought it up a couple more times, but I shot it down. I think he is disappointed and I know my mother is disappointed. She always told me he was a good man, a good soldier who loved his country, but when he took off his uniform, he was just another disrespected and mistreated black man, and that broke my father's heart."

"And what about you? Are you disappointed?" She asks, trying to use some of those empathetic questing skills that allow people to vent freely without judgment.

"Yeah, yeah, I am. I loved my father, but I feel like I deny his existence. Well, I know I am."

"Then, why do it? If it causes you and your family pain?"

Malcolm pauses and then looks over at Natasha, whose large brown eyes fixate on him. It is a question he asks himself often but never needs to answer out loud. Then again, no one knows this secret besides his family, so all of this is a first. He sighs, for he knows, revealing the truth out loud is painful. It is why he ignores the feelings of guilt.

"Because I wouldn't be here if I didn't lie about who I am. I wouldn't be allowed in the room, let along at the table. When I go to meetings with high powered accounts, there are usually no people of color or women in the room. They speak freely and openly about race and gender, and they have no intention of ever helping women or black people get a seat a the table."

"What about you? You helped me get a seat at the table." Tasha replies gratefully.

"I did it for me, too. The partners don't want to come off as an old racist firm, so I convinced them you would help improve their image, and in turn, we get more clients, and I get a promotion. So, in the end, I'm no better or worse than them."

"I don't think you're like them at all," She says, trying to sound sympathetic.

"Maybe, but I am like you. I mean, you lied to get here, too."

He turns to her and smiles. She looks down and away.

"It's ok, Natasha. I know. You don't have to hide anymore. I feel better, you know, tell you this all out loud. I feel lighter. I think you should do the same."

Tasha recounts the last year of her life, her career-ending, her best friend moving, and the desperation she felt, especially when she saw the flyer in the kitchen on one of her shifts. Malcolm listens intently as the pieces of the puzzles come together. She looks up and sees they are approaching the Lincoln Tunnel.

"Wait, you're taking me to Jersey? Why didn't you just drop me off at the train station?"

"Well, we were having a conversation. Plus, my family is in Jersey, I will crash there for the night. You live in Newark, right? What's your address, and I'll punch it in the GPS."

She tells him her address and the ride through the Lincoln Tunnel in silence. At this time of night, traffic is light, and they quickly drive through without issue. As they exit the tunnel, their conversation weighs heavily on her.

"What are you going to do now? Are you going to tell the partners about me?" She asks, concerned about her future.

Malcolm laughs, "Are you going to tell the partners about

me? We both have taken steps to get where we wanted. Look, you're talented and smart, and summer is almost over. Whatever you choose to do, you will be successful, and I am happy to be a reference for you, the real you, Natasha." He looks over at her, he can tell she is embarrassed by all this, but he can understand her perspective, so he tries to be gentle with his next question.

"So, Why did you choose to lie - change your age?

"Well, the jobs available now are either assistants or Vice Presidents, and my experience catches me in between. I'm too expensive for an assistant, and I don' have enough experience for a leadership position. Plus, I always get mistaken to be younger than I am, and I just stopped correcting people when they assume."

Well, you did not come across as a typical 20 year old. You carry yourself with such grace, even when you are telling off the partners for one of their tone-deaf ideas. You should have seen all their faces when you told Lakes, he follows through with that campaign, and he might as well change his name from Bob Lakes to Robert E. Lee." Malcolm tosses his head back and laughs, but he can tell Natasha is not amused. "Sorry." He quickly apologizes.

"He wanted to rebrand a small woman-owned custom textile company with a logo of a general on a horse and women laying around him in a cotton field. The whole thing screamed antebellum south. Plus the brand wants to support women artisans and revive the American textile industry, what does a man on a horse have to do with it?" Tasha throws her hands in the air, still upset over the thought of it "But I should not have said that last part. I cringe just thinking about it, but thank you for sticking up for me in that meeting. I appreciate it."

Malcolm pulls in front of Tasha's apartment and puts the car in park. "You're welcome. Anytime, ok. And don't ever stop speaking your mind. Too many people stay silent, and we need people like to call out the bullshit." He gives a small smile, and through the dim streetlights, she can almost see the green of his eyes.

"Well, it's a lot of work, and frankly, I can use some help, but can I give you some advice?" Tasha nervously asks, and Malcolm nods, giving her the signal to proceed.

"I've been lying about myself for two months, and talking about it tonight is a relief. I can finally breathe. I can't tell you what to do, and I'm not going to give you a speech on being 'black and proud' because, well, it's hard. Some days, I just want to be a person and not a black woman with the weight of my entire family, culture, and race on my shoulders when I enter the room. It would nice just to be myself, but what's the point of being in a position of privilege if you're not going to help others reach their potential. You should be calling out the racist and sexist BS. You should be advocating for more diversity in hiring, and if the partners don't want to listen, then screw it! You have an ivy league degree, you have connections and experience, and you can start your consulting firm and represent all those brands that are looking for a platform to be authentic! And you can do under your real name and as black men, because dammit its 2021 and people are just going have to be comfortable with black people being in the room!"

Tasha smacks her forehead for another one of her famous no filter rants.
"I apologize, I just get worked up, you know. Well, anyway, thanks for taking me home. Goodnight and have a nice weekend."

Malcolm reaches for Tasha's hand, and she stops opening the passenger side door.

"I admire your passion, Natasha. Never stop being you, and I try to start being me. The real me."

Malcolm's words linger as she exits the car.

Chapter 10

"Hey, Tasha, sorry we have to make this quick today. We have some potential investors coming in this afternoon, hence the herbal tea and not the rose!" Tina squeals as she tells Tasha all about her adventures these past couple weeks. The cannabis farm's strain to help with PTSD generated some interest, and investors provide funding for further research and testing!" Tasha is happy that Tina is doing something she loves and has the potential to help so many people. She only wishes she did the same thing this summer, instead of being selfish. They both have been super busy, so they missed a couple of Rose Saturdays, but they always try to pick back up where they left off.

"How's the freelance going? Any news if they are hiring full time?" Tina asks as she takes a bite of her vegan egg sandwich.

"Well, I want to talk to you about that. I know I should not have done it, but I lied to you and my parents."

"Well, it's not like you to lie, Tasha. You are more prone to bluntly telling the truth." Tina replies, concerned.

"Well, remember when I said I was feeling desperate, and I needed to take a risk and..."

"Yes," Tina replies sternly and not in her usual sing-songy voice.

Tasha explains the events over the past few weeks, going into detail to make sure not to leave anything out. Tina listens intently, trying to keep up with Tasha's frantic fast pace talking. Tasha expects Tina to be extremely disappointed in her.

"Well, Tasha, I was not expecting you to say that. But this does explain why you were so short with me every time I asked about it. And wow, I thought he had a secret love child, or maybe he was a government spy, but passing in the 21st century, wow." Tina says, not expecting juicy gossip this Saturday, but Malcolm fascinates her, and she wants to know more. Perhaps, she can spare some extra time for her dear friend.

"Yes, I'm not shocked, I suspected it. I know it's hard to tell from the sneaky stalker photos I sent you, but yes, Malcolm is one of us in disguise. Plus, people pass or pretend to be racial ambiguous all the time. It's not outdated. Just look at Instagram."

"That is true. It must be nice to "be Black" when it is convenient and profitable." Tina replies as she nods her head before sipping her tea.

"Anyway, the presentation is next week, and after that, I'm done being 22 years old. No more lying. I'm going to forget this ever happened and move forward."

"Tasha or Natasha, it's you. You are still here -or she. You lied about your age, but technically everything else is still you: your skills, your knowledge, your personality. I know you hate the name Natasha because you think it sounds like a Russian heiress and not a Black girl from Philly, but it's your name. Embrace it. Just be Natasha Worthington."

Somehow Tina had a way to spin things into a moment of reflection. When you ask Tina for advice, she always poses a question. She speaks in parables, and it can be quite annoying sometimes, especially when you just want a straight answer. Tasha is the straight shooter, and Tina is the philosopher. It's how their friendship works.

"Thank you, Christina." Tasha cheekily replies.

"Plus, Malcolm knows your secret, and you know his secret, so you two are bonded for life now. What are you going to do about him?

"Well, he said he would keep quiet, and I said the same thing. But if he chooses to tell Corey or the partners, well then that's it. Corey is his best friend. I imagine he will tell him everything. But that would mean the end of his career, so I really can't say."

"Well, Tasha, I have to say you outdid yourself this time, but as you always seem to get yourself into messes and magically back out of them."

"Except this time, the stakes are a bit higher than usual," Tasha replies, feeling deflated.

"Well, whatever happens, and whatever you decided to do, just be true to yourself. Ok, Tasha?" Tina asks lovingly

"If It's one thing I do well, it's to be myself, unapologetically! Cheers!" Tasha raises her glass of fine and clinks Tina's morning green tea through the computer screen.

The following week, Tasha keeps repeating Malcolm's words in her head. She knows her situation is slightly different than Malcolm's, but to her, lying is lying, and either way, she is not true to herself or her fellow interns. She is not in her early twenties anymore. Everyone wants a do-over, but sometimes you just have to build off whatever life throws at you. The way Malcolm looks at her makes her feels guilty. He sees her as innocent, but she feels just like a fraud as he does. The presentation is this Thursday, and then that's it, the internship is over, and the lies are over. Can she even put this on her resume? Will she have to live her life at Natasha, bubbly 22-year-old forever? When can she be Tasha again? What is the point of all this?. Once this week is over, she is shutting down this ruse for good. Tasha will still have the skills and the portfolio she built and can use that knowledge to find another job. She is resourceful, and she is a hustler, it will all work out. Eventually, the economy will turn around, and people will want to purchase expensive furniture and light fixtures. She just needs to be a little more patient, and as her mother says, "have a little more faith."

She walks into the office, feeling distracted. Immediately Jolene notices because she is intuitive and can sense when someone's vibes are off.

"Hey, Natasha, you ready to practice?" Spencer asks, interrupting Jolene's thoughts.

"Um, hey Spencer, yeah sure," Tasha replies distractedly

They walk into the conference room for another presentation run through. Tasha doesn't need her flashcards anymore since they practice so much. Jolene is meticulous, and she keeps the team together. Spencer improvises most of his part of the presentation as he is a natural-born talker or "bull shitter," as Tasha lovingly refers to him. Jolene sticks to the script, and she times her cues down to the second.

"Hey, Natasha, you seem distracted. Is everything ok?" Jolene asks as she pulls her to the side before entering the room.

"Jolene, I will reveal everything on Friday. I'm going to come clean. I must."

"No, it's fine. I know, you don't say anything, and I won't tell."

"You know?" Tasha asks curiously.

"Yes, you let some things slip over too much champagne. My mama always says champagne is a truth serum!" They both laugh, and Spencer stares at annoyingly.

"What are you two laughing at?

"Girl Talk!" Jolene shouts back.

Over the second half of the summer, the three of them have bonded over the grunt work of being interns. While they are working on a presentation, most of the time, they assist Malcolm, Corey, and the partners with supporting tasks, which can be anything from copying and stapling to help put together graphics for million-dollar accounts. She is happy that she finally gets along with Spencer, and she and Jolene are much closer now. However, Tasha feels guilty for betraying their trust, and she is surprised that Jolene is so understanding of the situation. They do not have time to discuss it. It's a small office, and someone is always listening, besides they have to run through their presentation for the hundredth time!

Malcolm quietly sits in his office, drinking his coffee like he does every morning. Corey walks in abruptly and shuts the door.

"You want to tell me about these?" Corey slams down grainy security photos of him and Tasha standing by his car. The timestamp reads 11:07 pm.

"She was helping me finish a project for the Murphy Account. It was late, and I gave her a ride home. That's it."

"That's it? I'm your best friend. You can tell me if something is going on?" Corey huffs.

"Nothing is going on. I promise you. And why do you have those?"

"Ok, well be careful, because girls like her are always looking for a way in." Corey dances around the question, sits down in an empty office chair.

"What does that mean?" Malcolm asks sternly, already knowing the answer to the question, but wants to hear Corey's explanation.

"She is not a good fit here. I mean, she does good work, and she is very talented, but she doesn't fit the company culture."

"Doesn't fit the company culture." Malcolm scoffs because he know it is code for 'you're not white enough to work here.'

"The only reason she is here is because you vouched for her, and they respect your judgment. They understand that this was to gives us a better look on the diversity front and along with donating to those charities you suggested. Our image is improving, and we are starting to get new clients. But she rubs the partners the wrong way."

Malcolm interrupts Corey. "What about her rubs the partners the wrong way?"

Malcolm looks up. Usually, when Corey comes into his office to vent, he continues working away, nodding at the appropriate moments and saying, 'oh man, that sucks' to comfort him through any grievances. Corey usually complains about the generational clash between him and his father. Malcolm is often a go-between, and it can be rather exhausting keeping the peace between the Waters men. However, today he is complaining about the interns, Natasha, in particular, and this irks Malcolm. SO far this summer, Corey's interest in the interns consists of him playing the cool Uncle, while Malcolm supervises their daily tasks and monitors everyone progress. He assumes the internship is another way for Corey to show face and not do any real work. So why is he picking on Natasha? Malcolm thinks but does comment any further.

"You know, look, she doesn't have the education or the breeding to understand the work we do here. I already talked to Dad. At the end of the summer, we will hire Jolene and Spencer. I'm sure you can write her a good letter of recommendation. So you did a good job, so just let her go. It's for the best

"Breeding! We are talking about a woman, not a bog. Damn Corey. And she is a designer who went to design school? I do not see the issue here!" Malcolm raises his voice, which is not usual, and Corey looks surprised.

"Mal, she is opinionated and doesn't know her place. Did you see the way she grilled Lakes in our company meeting a couple of weeks ago? He felt disrespected."

"She had valid questions and concerns that none of us ever thought of. That's what diversity is important in the workplace." Malcolm says as he tries to compose himself.

" Look, I'm sure we can find a way to make our workplace more diverse without upsetting the balance of things. The partners are old school, and they want things done a certain way."

"So Corey, as per my understanding, you admit Natasha does amazing work, you admit that her skills and her mere presence here has benefited the business, but we are going to hire the two interns who are here on favors?" Malcolm stares at Corey, who fidgets with his hands and remains quiet.

"And the partners agree to this? I don't have a say in the

matter?" Malcolm retorts as he tries not to sound too defensive.

"Everyone is on the same page." Corey hesitates and waits for Malcolm's response, but Malcolm just turns his chair away from Corey.

Malcolm sat furiously at his computer and is appalled at the audacity of Corey. They have disagreements like all friends do, but this feels different. Something is amiss, and something sneaky is going on. How dare Corey storm into his office talking about Natasha is "not a culture fit." This fight is the last straw. All will be revealed on Friday.

Chapter 11

The morning of the presentation starts according to the plan. Tasha sets her alarm extra early to have time to take a long meditative shower, eat a hearty breakfast, and have a soothing cup of tea. She also wants to get to the office early. The presentation is scheduled for 10 am, and by her calculations, she should walk into the office promptly at 8:27 am. Jolene had lent one of her mom's vintage Chanel black sheaths for the occasion gifted her with a new pair of block-heeled Tory Burch shoes, her favorite brand. Usually, she does not accept such an extravagant gift, but she now knows how much Jolene's family is worth, she no longer feels guilty. She put the shoes in her tote and slipped into her sneakers for the commute.

As she left her house and walks to the train station, she receives a text from Spencer in the intern group chat.

Spencer: "SOS – presentation moves to 8 am. Sorry. Long story. Please forgive me. They just sent an email."

Jolene: "You ass! What did you do? I'm getting dressed, and my driver is on his way."

Natasha: "Um, what?????"

Spencer: "Sorry, I made a joke to Corey, back when we were enemies - not frienemies, that wouldn't it be funny to change the time at the last minute so you would be late. I didn't know he listened!"

Jolene: "SPENCER – THE DEVIL IS GONNA GET YOU!!!"

Jolene: "Natasha, where are you? What can we do to help?"

Natasha: "They delayed due to some problems in the tunnel. I have to run. I'm going to be late. If I am on schedule, I will arrive at 8:30 at the earliest."

Spencer: …

Jolene: "Ok, I'll have my driver pick you up from Penn station after he drops me off. I'll give you my driver's number so you can contact him when you arrive. So sorry!"

Spencer: "I'm so so so so sorry. I'll speak to Corey and smooth this all over."

Natasha: "It's okay. I'll see you when I get there. Just stall your part of the presentation until I can come in. I'll text you when I get to the office."

Spencer: "So, SORRY. Promise to make it up to you!" His last texts consists of ten or so random heart emojis. I guess that's his way of saying sorry.

Tasha puts her phone in her purse and stares at the train monitor at Newark Penn Station. She surveys her options, and the last minute decides to jump on the PATH trains, which by an out of the way route, will get her to midtown NYC. She runs onto the train before the door closes and squeezes in. Masks on public transit is still the norm, but since more people are back to work than in the previous months, everyone packs the trains. There is nowhere to sit, and this wool-blend dress does not go well with August. Tasha surprises herself for not being angry at this situation. She realizes that her luck is going run out eventually. At this point, Tasha prays that the public transportation systems have mercy on her and deliver her on time. She's not upset with

Spencer, they had made amends, but Corey. He is always friendly and complementary. She has plenty of emails with him praising her work. Why would he sabotage her like this? A thought flashed in her mind -Malcolm! She shouts his name out loud unintentionally, and fellow passengers give quick annoyed glances. He must know about Malcolm.

Malcolm walks into the conference room and looks around sees everyone but Natasha. He starts to get concerned. He looks over at the interns, Jolene is frantically texting, and Spencer is the corner schmoozing Corey. He takes his seat and greets the other partners. Corey gives him a wry smile before giving a brief introduction.

"Hello, everyone, we are going to get started. Thank you for attending this presentation for the summer of 2021 interns. Our first internship program since 2011, when the amazing, always honest, always virtuous Malcolm joined the family. We are so pleased to have all of you here and so proud of our three interns. Oh," Corey pauses and looks around the room. "There seems to be one intern missing. I guess she partied too hard last night."

A chorus of laughter explodes from the partners, and Jolene gives a concerned look to Spencer. Corey provides a wry smile toward Malcolm, but he is not amused. All Spencer interrupts Corey's speech and reveals is that Natasha's part of the presentation requires a grand entrance, so everything is going accordingly to plan. However, Corey did not seem to care, and it almost seems he is happy that his last-minute email switch up is working as intended. Spencer feels uneasy about the entire situation, and he is just hoping this all pans out.

Corey finishes his speech and takes a seat between Malcolm and his father, Charles Waters.

"Was that necessary?" Malcolm whispers to Corey. "That was an ass move."

"Well, we need someone who can afford a car and doesn't have to take the bus. These things happen, and she needs to be available and flexible, this just proves it."

"We're you always a racist, elitist, sexist prick?" Malcolm whispers back, and before Corey can respond, Jolene, sensing the rising tension in the room, promptly begins the presentation.

Spencer knows that Jolene is methodical in her approach and her portion of the presentation about the financials of the company and how their profit can increase if they invest more money in technology, especially their app, takes precisely 14 minutes, not a second more. So, it is up to him to drag out the marketing and advertising strategy of the presentation, so it smoothly transitions into Natasha's highly anticipated part of the display. Jolene wraps up her slides and Spencer transitions.

Tasha's sweat is a combination of stress and the lack of air circulation on the train. Of all the days for this to happen. The train approaches the stop, and she rushes out sprinting through the turnstile and up the stairs. Tasha receives a message from Jolene's driver stating there is a protest happening, and he can't get through to midtown. Tasha is not surprised, whether it's climate change, Black Lives Matters, or women's reproductive rights there has been protests in New York City non stop since the pandemic last year. However, it annoys her that so many people want to protest at 8 am. Never the less, she rushes through the crowds and makes her way to the subway. She checks her phone, and the time is 8:22.

Spencer might as well do a magic show. He is starting to get nervous and begins to tell corny jokes. He receives some hearty chuckles from the partners but looks over at Corey and Malcolm, and they are not smiling. He imagines they can smell the bullshit. He continues to go through his slides, he never actually writes anything down and just speaks off the top of his head, but his anxiousness is making him stumble a bit. He must keep it together for Natasha. After all, this is his fault she is in this predicament.

Tasha skips a few steps and catches the subway uptown. Another passenger who notices the stress on her face stuck his foot out to delay the doors closing - a brief moment of New York solidarity. She decides to take a deep breath. At this point, she is moving as fast as humanly possible during the morning rush hour commute during a human rights protest. She checks her phone, it's 8:33, and she knows Spencer is doing his best to stretch out the presentation, and he can talk as the day is long, but everyone has their limits. Tasha sprints off the subway and scales the steps from the platform like a mountain climber. She hits the streets and bobs and weaves through pedestrians like a running back. "I am LeSean McCoy. I am Brian Westbrook." She thinks as she tries to avoid a group of tourists taking pictures, she cuts through the grass and immediately feels something squishy and smelly. Tasha looks down and sees the dog poop on the bottom of her sneakers. The smell hits her instantly, but she can't slow down. Tasha needs to make a decision, and this morning seems to be all about split-second decisions. A stranger hands her a plastic bag, she takes off her sneakers using the bag as a glove and throws them in the trash. These were the same sneakers she wore when Tina picked her up from the train station a year ago. Tina hates these shoes and will think it is divine intervention that they are ruined by Central Park dog poop on her last day of internship that she lied to get. Tasha hobbles to a park bench and puts on her 4 inch Tory Burch pumps. She needs to break these in, and can barely move in these shoes. The last part of her walk to the office is going to be painful. Tasha takes a step, and she rolls her ankle as soon as she begins to walk. They made these shoes for standing and looking pretty, not aggressive speed walking. She tries to pick up the pace as the clock is ticking.

    Corey begins to rise to speak. "Thank you, Spencer, I think it's time to wrap up…"

    Spencer feels the buzz of his phone in his back pocket and interrupts Corey. "Ladies and gentlemen, I pass this over to Natasha."

    Tasha bursts through the door in stride in her 4-inch heels.

Spencer passes her the laser pointer, and Jolene dims the lights. The next 15 minutes included a laser show, a question and answer section, and an interactive mobile game. It is a last-minute idea to spruce up the final part of their presentation, and the interns spent the last week working on it. They want to show the partners how much technology is available to do a pitch, and you do not have to rely on just slides and a laser pointer anymore. At one point, Spencer looks over at her, and she gives him a wink. Overall, they think this presentation is a success. For a brief moment, Natasha locks eyes with Malcolm, he looks proud, but Corey seems pissed. She wraps up the presentation, and all the partners stand in applause. Corey's mouth drops open, and Malcolm's lips curl up a little, which she counts as a smile.

The partners and supervisors congratulate the interns and shake their hands.

"Congratulations, Natasha. Well Done." Corey extends his hand, and Tasha shakes it, relieved that this whole ordeal is almost over. Corey lingers, holds her hand tighter, and leans in to whisper, "On your 2010 Pennsylvania State High School Softball Championship."

Tasha's eyes widen, and Malcolm notices this exchange from across the boardroom. She swears she cross-checked everything, social media, bank records, and even those creepy stalker websites and her computer whiz friend does not make mistakes. Then suddenly she remembers her hacker friend asking about any fun facts or interesting talents, or awards, because that always gives people away. High school is so far in the past, she did not think to mention her stint as a star pictcher of her high school softball team. Corey probably has a team that can search through 500 or so pages on the internet just to find this one article and team photo. However, he does not look like a man who is short on resources. A rush of anxiety overwhelms her as he backs away. Malcolm tries to weave his way toward Natasha, but he is interrupted when Hilda comes in with bottles of champagne and orange juice.

"I hope it's not too early for mimosas." Hilda cheers and everyone claps in unison.

They all take a glass, and Corey proposes a toast.

"Well, great summer to all the interns, and you truly are essential to the team. Jolene, you were brilliant as always, a true shining star." Jolene blushes at this compliment. "Spencer, you kept everyone laughing and on their toes. We look forward to all the wonderful things you will do next. And Natasha, our wildcard, even though some of us were skeptical of having you here, you proved you were "worthy" of the position." The partners laugh at play on words, and Tasha guesses that the best compliment she is going to get, and hopes that is all he has to say.

However, Corey continues, "I have an amusing story about how Natasha landed this internship. As you know, my good friend Malcolm vouched for her credentials." A sense of dread comes over Tasha as a feeling of amusement shines across Corey's face. "However," Corey continues but is interrupted abruptly by Malcolm.

"Thank you, Corey. And what he was trying to say is, ten years ago, you all took a chance on me and look at me now. So I wanted to pay it forward, as it goes, and allow Natasha to have the same opportunities I had. So, she is not our traditional choice, but neither am I. We have so much in common, like the fact we both Black, talented, and passionate about our work. Corey offered me a seat at the table when no one else would, and for that, I am forever grateful."

Malcolm addresses his past, speaks about his father and his eventual death. He talks about how his denying his heritage allows him to enter restricted spaces.

"The only person who knows my story Corey, and despite that, he is my best friend. He kept his promise to stay quiet until I was ready. It's through meeting Natasha and learning more about her, that I realized it's time for me to be myself. I've enjoyed my time here at Lakes, Rivers, and Waters, but it is time for me to move on."

Gasps around the room and the partners give each other strange looks. Charles Waters looks at Corey, angry at being blindsided by this information.

Malcolm continues. "I am going to start a new consulting fir- Malcolm Johnson Banks Consulting," Malcolm pauses and gives a huge smile at Natasha, before continuing, "A frim where diversity is at the forefront. My first hire is a graduate of Drexel University, class of 2014, Natasha Worthington. What do you say? Would you like to work with me?"

Tasha's mouth gapes open, and Malcolm's sticks out his hand. Jolene practically pushes her into Malcolm, and Spencer claps in celebration. She chugs her champagnes and shouts, "Yes, of course!"

Corey is still in shock of the news that his best friend is half-Black, lied about it all these years, and then told his father that he knew all of long. Corey has the prestige and charm, but Malcolm manages to outwit him every time. The partners storm out of the conference room. Charles Waters turns around and demands an audience with his son. Corey shakes his head at Malcolm. "You were always better at the long game, Mal," before walking out of the room.

Tasha and Malcolm continue to celebrate in the conference room with the other interns.

"Wait, Natasha, you're like 30?" Spencer crows.

"I'm 29, Spencer, so not yet." Tasha lovingly snaps back.

"Jolene, you knew and Malcolm, you knew?"

"We figured it out." Malcolm and Jolene say in unison.

"My Mama always says Champagne is a truth serum, ain't that right, Natasha." Jolene jokes.

"That's right, Jolene! And my friends call me Tasha so you can call me that too."

"Well, Tasha." Malcolm smiles. "We start on Monday."

JAZZMEEN UNDERWOOD

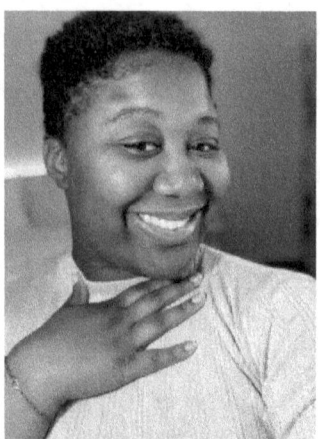

Jazzmeen Underwood

"My work is a commitment to self-love and discovery. As a writer, it is important for me to share my words in a way that relates to others who may feel the same. I aspire to inspire those who seek clarity through art. I write for those who may not find the words when they need it."

Stage Left

I want to be free within my own right
I'd rather move to my own groove
I no longer seek your approval
No longer valid for you.

KOI KIZZIE

Untitled

Silence is the greatest tune.
Silence in the mind
When we embrace this, we can hear ourselves
"I AM AT PEACE WITH YOU"
Can you introduce me to solitude?
we have some bonding to do.

Mighty & Swift

There is life that resides
in your colorful mind
Fast paces & many places
that you have been

Do not doubt your strength
Do not question your glory
because every answer lies within

Trust yourself
Trust your soul
You've known of your power

Now, believe it

Inhale your grace
Exhale your doubt
Your life is yours
Now weather your storm....

Conversations with Nature

As the winds blow,
The trees speak
The shadows lurk and the birds screech
"let me tell you a story", said the friendly ghost
"May I have this dance?", asked the moving branches
Bare feet to earth, I resonate
I love you and the power you invest in me
Can I be of myself?
What's it like to tune out the world and tune into you?
What about the power you exude?
The timeless beauty you possess
What can their opinions do?
All that matters is you.

- Alsoknownasshe

EDDIE WHITE

Eddie White is a Memphis-born artist, writer and rapper— in that order. He has been drawing since kindergarten and writing stories since the second grade, with rapping coming into his life around fourth grade. With all three, he's found inspiration in comic books, manga, light novels and various forms of animation. His story, 'The Ballad of Otieno', is a unique take on the vampire mythos with parallels to religion, racism and interracial relationships. While the included part is only the first half, the entire story is meant to be an allegory on the aforementioned subjects. When not writing, drawing or working on music, he divides his time between researching, odd-jobbing, reading, binging anime and gaming.

The Ballad on Otieno: Part 1

DAILY I THIRST, thirst for peace and sleep. Loathing this anguished state of mind I have been burdened with. Constantly feeling the strain of being heartbroken and melancholy. I wasn't always this way though. No, I used to be full of life and optimistic. Every day was a joyous occasion. And what a magnificent blessing it was to be alive, especially as long as Cantrelle was by my side.

Yes, as long as I had Cantrelle, I could overcome anything.

She was my everything. The woman I shared all of my life-long goals with as well as my passions and fears. The one I wanted to be unified with, forever and a day, but she was snatched out of my—NO—she was RIPPED from my arms. STOLEN from my embrace. TAKEN from my heart in the blink of an eye. And the magic we created, an additional magnificent blessing that was growing inside of her, was taken as well.

That's right, Cantrelle was pregnant when her precious life was snuffed out by those heartless fiends. Those lascivious, infernal, bloodthirsty mongrels I once called brothers. The brothers I once fought side by side with in countless wars and skirmishes. Those malignant sows whom I put my ass on the line for time and time again.

Those godforsaken demons known by many as Vampires.

***

As much as I hate to admit it, I'm a Vampire too, but I'm not like them and have vowed that I would never become such. However, during the time of my grief, I became something a lot worse. Something a lot more sinister and depraved than they'd ever be.

After the incident which befell my sweet Cantrelle, vengeance became my coping mechanism and I ran rampant through my village of Malhela, leaving nothing but death and destruction in my wake. I was soon branded both a predator and a pariah to my own kind as my particular taste in victims became more widely known.

How did I acquire such a status, you ask? Well, I sought out and kidnapped the wives and girlfriends of my brethren and murdered them, but not before checking for a certain—How can I say it?—PREREQUISITE.

That prerequisite was pregnancy.

Once I knew for certain they were with child, I bared my fangs and dug in, draining all the blood I could from their bodies. And since the blood of pregnant Vampires has a distinct quality, I became a beast of an entirely different nature. Everything about me changed as a result of the blood I ingested. And as far as I know, these changes are permanent.

My vicious and indiscriminate feeding caused a mutation in my genetic makeup, which also altered me physically. One change in particular made my eyes a deep and glossy black, while the irises within became a pinkish purple. Richly hued and markedly radiant, it has been said that staring into them is like peering into an orchid-colored inferno of souls.

Now that I've had time to dwell on it, it's quite frightening and sends chills through every bone in my cursed body knowing all that innocent blood is coursing inside of me. Or rather, WAS coursing inside of me.

Still, I am a bottle of emotions, assorted like vitamins. Sometimes I feel wrath, sometimes terror and, more often than not, I feel animus. But currently, I strongly feel remorseful.

Yes, I am remorseful.

And I guess it would be fitting that I'd feel remorse for my actions with my death certain and impending. Surely that thought has run through the minds of all headed for execution before. I know I'm not alone. Regret and compassion in this instance are normal.

I am more than aware that I deserve the death which awaits me. I gleefully welcome it actually. Cognizance of my wrongs is obvious, but were those who trespassed against me not also culpable? Were they not driven by hearts full of malice when they slayed my dear Cantrelle? Why is it that my act of vengeance is the only sin my brethren see?

There may be a plank in my eye, but there are logs in theirs, and the fact that they ignore how I was wronged really irritates me. I must digress though, as two wrongs can never make a right. What I did was unforgivable, so I do not expect mercy to be shown. I never expected that at all. What I did expect was understanding. Is there anybody willing to grant me that much at least?

†††

Due to my current state of pensive observation, I neglected to mention that I have been locked-up—shackled actually—in the cellar of an old church located in Malhela. And before I go any further, Malhela is a village located in this grand land of Kätek.

Kätek exists parallel to the entire world and has done so for centuries. It's actually been around since the dawn of time, but the meteor that hit and caused the Ice Age forced it inside of a rip in the fabric of the universe. It is a special place that's home to not only us Vampires, but Goblins, Werewolves, Aetherkind (Angels), the Inferabla (Demons) and tons of other mythical beings.

We've all been living in secret, keeping our home cloaked from the nosy "para-dwelts" (people who live on the opposite side of the veil). Occasionally though, they get the notion to explore places they shouldn't and find one of the entrances, eventually becoming breakfast, lunch or dinner for the denizens of our hideaway.

Anyway, for four weeks now I've been bound in this church where they've drained blood from me so that I can become weakened. To this end, they have taken blades made of pure silver infused with cosalabast (a cosmic variety of alabaster) and covered them in goblin venom, which is highly lethal to Vampires. They pierced my side—as that Roman soldier did Jesus—and slashed my flesh all over, from head to toe. Once enough of my strength is depleted, I'll be powerless to fight back.

I never planned to fight any of this even though a fire burns inside of me to slaughter all of my so-called brethren.

But yes—I was always willing to accept my fate, that's why I allowed myself to be caught. I did it because I know the guilty can't evade justice forever, but also because I don't want to live a life without Cantrelle. Without her, survival seems pointless. Some will claim that I can always find love again, but finding love as a Vampire isn't so black and white. Not everyone is willing to trade their mortality and live for an eternity, and I don't exactly blame them.

It would seem becoming immortal should be an easy choice, but the finalizing of such a life-altering decision requires massive deliberation. It took Cantrelle five years to agree to it, but it was five years where I didn't mind waiting for an answer. As long as her choice came from a place of sincerity, she could've taken ten years to do so.

I am understanding of the extended wait times because this is a pretty heavy subject to move forward on. It requires one's heart to be in the right place in order to decide they want it. Becoming a Vampire means outliving everybody you love and care about. It means moving from place to place and changing your identity so as to not arouse suspicion. It means avoiding being photographed and filmed.

And just for the record, that was a falsehood they spread claiming we aren't visible in mirrors, photos and film. We're very visible, but just go out of our way to not be seen, hence why Kätek still exists.

Still, a majority of us spend more time on the other side than we do there. We find places to stay, hold down jobs, go clubbing and pretty much get involved in almost all human activities. We often end up hiding in plain sight, biding our time until we can feed. And whenever we do feed, it's done so in a meticulous manner. At least eighty-five percent of the time we exhibit a great degree of control over our hunger. However, there's still that fifteen percent where those amongst us get consumed by bloodlust. In addition to all of that, we aren't "harmed" by sunlight like books, films and television say. We avoid the sun because it reveals our true nature. God does not like us, even though He created us, so He cursed our vampiric visage to be seen during daylight. That "burning" you often see depicted in entertainment is an over-exaggeration.

This is why we work at night though, for it would be quite the sight if a long-eared, four-horned and fanged grey-skinned creature just came waltzing into Best Buy on a Monday morning ready to clock-in. That wouldn't be kosher in the slightest. It would honestly be extremely horrifying and make children scream like banshees as they wet themselves while the elderly turn mortified, resulting in heart attacks.

Nothing about that scenario is pretty.

Sorry, I didn't mean to wander about and speak on my kind, I only meant to discuss my forthcoming execution and how I am more than willing to go through with it. At this point, I don't think there's much else to say. Besides, I just heard the door to the cellar open, it appears it is time.

***

The wooden door opened with a cackling creak and a beam of bright moonlight shot inside via a hole in the wall of the church. It immediately struck me in my weary eyes which had been fed nothing but total darkness for the past twenty-eight days. I must admit though that it felt good to finally have a form of lumination upon my face, especially in my weakened state.

Not long after opening the door, a giant, burly, bald-headed individual with a woolly salt-and-pepper beard walked in. He was clad entirely in an armored black outfit with gold and purple trimmings, black finger-less gloves and heavy black combat boots. He had a rather swarthy appearance to his skin and his eyes were two different colors, with his right eye an icy steel grey color, while his left one was milky white and opaque as matte stoneware. Lastly, over his left eye was a darkened scar, worn and blending with the wrinkles decorating his face.

From his size and apparel, I gathered he was a member of Alphacrat Nosphero's branch of the Imperial Agonizers. He particularly loves those physically imposing Viking-like brutes.

For the record, the Imperial Agonizers—or Im-Ags for short—are a regiment of the most elite Vampires in service to the Alphacrat Council. They rank high in nobility and never venture outside of the capital of Kätek unless they absolutely have to. With that being said, this man wouldn't be here if Nosphero didn't have bigger plans.

The big guns are never brought out for a mere fly. It's either going to be a grand display to make an example out of me, or something else entirely. I pray for the former.

†††

As I twitch and heave while shackled to the wall, reeling from my state of dolor, the gigantic man approaches.

"Otieno Benedict. I am Piaras Tor. You have been charged with the following crimes perpetrated against our kind: Kidnapping, voluntary manslaughter and engaging in sexual relations with an Aetherkind. How do you plead?"

"I plead guilty."

Piaras widens his eyes in surprise. "No resistance, young man? I must say, I'm impressed, but also disappointed. Expected you to put up at least some semblance of a fight. Tch."

"I have no desire to fight this, I just want to get it over with. So please, can you hurry it along?"

"My dear boy, there's no need to rush. You'll meet your end soon enough," Piaras replies in a raspy tone as he lightly slaps my cheek. "Besides, I'm just getting started, so I suggest you get comfortable."

"It's rather hard to do that when I've been chained up for four weeks!" I exclaim as I lunge forward.

I knew I would be hindered by the shackles binding me, but I kept trying to attack him. Piaras just laughed though at my scarred, emaciated body squirming to get free. To him, I probably looked like a chihuahua on a leash trying to intimidate an elephant. I swear, if I could've willed myself free, I would've done so. But alas, I was too weak from having a majority of my strength bled away.

"Four weeks is nothing, Otieno. We can make this last for centuries. It's best you mind your tongue."

"What the... ... ...centuries?!"

In anger, I lunged forward one final time, but Piaras caught me by the throat with his massive gloved right hand. He lifted me off the ground and started squeezing it so hard that I thought he'd crush my windpipe. He gave a big grin, his fanged teeth showing through that fluffy beard of his as he stared me straight in the eyes while I choked.

A flood of tears arose as I began wheezing and coughing almost simultaneously. It had seemed as though my death would come quicker than expected, but eventually he let me go.

"I should just snap your little scrawny neck right now, but I have my orders. Can't disobey."

"Tool."

"Better than being a blasphemer."

"I'm not a blasphemer," I replied. "They took my love away from me. Why drag this out? Haven't I suffered enough?"

Enraged, Piaras slugs me in the chest then screams, "Don't you talk to me about suffering, boy! Did you think of that when you feasted upon our women?! No! You harbored nary a thought as such, so quit with the ploys for sympathy. They succumb to deafened ears here."

"I don't seek any fuckin' sympathy you old fool! I just wish to be with Cantrelle again. Please...Just grant me the death I desire and deserve so I can rest in peace."

Piaras grunted, "You poor, pathetic, contemptible Aetherphile." —he sniffs up and down my neck then grimaces in disgust— "You still smell like the bitch. Putrid."

Beyond irate from his statements, I took the opportunity while Piaras was close to headbutt him with all the strength I could muster, my forehead connecting with his wide nose, creating a sanguine geyser. I attempted to catch a drop of his blood as it sprayed, but it only landed on my face.

"You insolent cretin!" Piaras reacts, covering his nose to try and hinder the blood gushing out. "You're gonna pay for that!"

With his free hand, he backhands me with such force that I thought my neck would snap. Instead, my dreadlocks just scattered as the back of my head collided with the rough stone wall, leaving my cranium pounding away like twenty jackhammers.

I shook my head to try and alleviate the throbbing, but that wasn't the best idea, as the pain became worse. I'm hoping I don't have a concussion, as I wouldn't be able to heal from it properly in this state.

"You... ... ...you gigantic-ass ape... ... ...don't EVER disrespect the name of the woman I love like that again! Or I'll—"

Piaras cut me off with a fit of hearty laughter.

"Or you'll WHAT, Otieno?! What's your pathetic-ass gonna do to ME—Piaras Tor—in your current state?"

"Trust, if I wasn't shackled and had my full strength, I'd rip your fucking heart clean out then stomp on it," I growled.

Piaras raised his hand and wiggled his bloody fingers at me, "Ooooh, spooky. HA! Don't make me laugh, you sick freak. You know, they say you were once highly respected amongst us, but I wouldn't know it just by looking at you right now. Such a pity you went and fucked it all up. Tsk tsk."

Yeah, he's right, I was once respected. Until I fell in love with Cantrelle, then I immediately lost my status.

"I didn't fuck shit up, you guys just can't get your heads out of your asses for one nanosecond to see how much the world's changed."

"Nonsense! The world may have changed, but us Vamps NEVER DO! You were supposed to respect the Covenant!"

Yeah... the "Covenant".

At this point, I've zoned out as he continues to rave about that ancient piece of parchment full of outdated, garbage beliefs. That same parchment which said that Cantrelle and I could never be, but we never gave any fucks. We defied those rules, even at the risk of facing unified condemnation. If it's one thing a majority of Vampires and Aetherkind agreed on, it's that we are never supposed to mix. To do so was blasphemy and an abomination, punishable by death.

My love and I both knew the risks, yet we continued because we hoped our union would set an example. We STRIVED to show that having relations outside of our species presented no danger, but our detractors refused to grasp that.

***

Judging by the clock on the wall (which I could finally see), about fifteen minutes had gone by and the air of the whole room was full of so much tension that I thought we'd suffocate. After Piaras had finished lambasting me for not respecting the Covenant, I just stayed quiet. I didn't have much to say. Nothing he'd give a fuck to hear anyway. All I kept thinking in my head was 'Fuck the Covenant'.

Yeah—Fuck the Covenant.

It had done nothing but ruin my life. It had ruined all of our lives, whether many wanted to admit it or not. Still, everybody lived by it and couldn't dream of ever going against it. Cantrelle and I dared to do so though, and she paid with her life. I will join her soon in death, as the price for our romance required both souls to be spent.

"Enough of this silence! Talk! Answer for your dishonor, cretin!"

I took a deep breath and sighed. "I don't have much to say, Piaras. I mean, what do you expect? For me to beg for mercy and forgiveness? To express I'll change and uphold this 'precious' Covenant we have? Hmm?"

Piaras's face suddenly turned from ire to smugness.

"Well, if you repent, something could be arranged." —he began unlocking the shackles around my wrists— "As I said before, you were highly respected once. Nosphero would grant you clemency if you solemnly swore to abide by the laws as they are written."

"I'd rather die."

"Humph, figures," Piaras shrugs as he removes the shackles from my ankles. "Did you really love that wicked creature that much that you'd turn your back on everything you were taught?"

With the shackles gone, I'm struggling to stand, so I have myself a seat on the cold and dusty cellar floor.

"Sometimes what we're taught is wrong," I pause as I position myself against the wall for support so that I could massage my terribly aching ankles and legs. "It prohibits freedom of thought and inhibits being expressive. And yes: I did love her that much, but she's not a 'wicked creature'. She's a saint."

"That's not what the books say about her kind," Piaras replies as he walks over to a faucet (When did that get here?) and fills up a glass of water. He brings it to me and says, "Here. Drink up. I'm sure you're parched."

His kindness is shocking to say the least, especially after wanting to rip my head in two not that long ago. He must be hoping he can win me over to their side again, but he won't. That's impossible considering what those heartless fucks did.

"The books say a lot of bullshit," I respond, taking another pause to guzzle the glass of water as I am—indeed—parched. "You can't take it all at face value."

Piaras's facial expression returned to a soured one upon hearing my words. "If I were you, I wouldn't call the word of the Creator 'bullshit', young man. You best mind your tongue."

"You mean the same Creator who cursed us all and set about causing plagues and disasters every time He got pissed the fuck off?" I retort. "Yeah, nah. No thank you. Still bullshit to me."

No sooner had I said that did Piaras kick me square in the left side of my ribs. I heard a slight crack upon the impact of his heavy boots. I soon fell over, wincing in helpless distress.

"I SAID YOU BEST WATCH YOUR TONGUE, AETHERPHILE!" he yelled angrily as saliva flung from his mouth. "NEVER disrespect our Creator!"

I writhed in agony on the floor clutching my ribs. This hurts worse than when he backhanded me. Jesus fuckin' Christ. If I wasn't a Vamp, that kick would've killed me.

"The fuck you got in those boots—meteors?" I asked with great pain in my voice.

I tried to make light of the situation, but Piaras—upon composing himself—didn't even crack a smile. Guess he doesn't find me particularly amusing. What a tough crowd.

"You have little to no respect for what you are and where you come from. You lack the simple concept of how important it is to always be on code and honor your lineage. We didn't get this far being freethinkers."

I scoffed at his attempt to scold me. Where exactly does he get off saying such things?

"Tch. Yeah, it would seem you guys don't think at all. It's like a hive-mind."

"You're sadly mistaken, Otieno."

"I beg to differ. Show me where I'm wrong."

"Well, first of all, what you fail to understand is that we are not and have never been a monolith, but on that same note, we've never been ragtag. We are individuals who operate as units because it's what nature intends."

"Maaaaan—FUCK nature. You can kiss my bloodsucking ass with that shit. Anyway, I thought you were supposed to take me to get executed? Or torturing me. I mean, whichever it is, it's high time you get on with it."

"You're really in a rush to die, aren't you?" Piaras inquires with a chuckle.

"Yes. There's nothing left for me in this world."

"That's not true. What about your brethren?" —he takes a seat in front of me— "We're still here for you despite your crimes. Albeit, I'm not too keen on forgiving you, but I can look past it all if you were to repent."

"There you go with that nonsense again," I replied, shaking my head. "Repentance. Psssht! I'm not doing that shit."

"Why are you so determined to deny the Covenant, boy? Explain that to me."

"There's nothing to explain," I said. "What's been done has been done, what's been said has been said—I am who I am. Now please, can we finally get this over with?"

Piaras closed his eyes briefly and smiled before rising to his feet. "Fine then. As you wish."

***

Piaras guided me out of the cellar and into the church, where he stopped to place a silver collar with cosalabast rocks and amethyst gems in it around my neck. It's meant to keep my movements bound to being non-combative, but I highly doubt Piaras saw me as a threat.

"Is this really necessary?" I ask, pointing to the collar.

"I think you know the answer to that question, young man."

"Well, I'm not exactly in an optimal condition to fight, ya' know? I'm lightheaded, hungry and still thirsty."

Piaras points at his nose and grunts, "This blight on my face says otherwise."

I chuckled as I examined his nose, which is still swollen and bruised from the headbutt I gave him. "Eh, yeah……about that……my bad. Didn't know I had that much strength left."

Piaras didn't say a word, he just put a pair of cuffs on me (something else I didn't need) and walked me out of the church where I discovered it had been raining, making the hilltop that the church sat on very soggy and muddy. He walked me to a carriage at the bottom of it where I was "greeted"—very warmly I shall add—by two other Im-Ags who had been standing guard.

And when I say "greeted", I mean that I was beaten down.

And when I say beaten down, I mean that I was kicked, punched and stomped on until Piaras told them it was enough, which was only when it seemed like I was near-death.

After I endured that horrific attack, he lifted me up by my chin and tossed me inside of a cage that was built into the back of the carriage. The carriage, with its matte black paint job and crimson targa top, was hitched to two Guepusus, which are creatures native to Kätek that are like horses hybridized with cheetahs. They move incredibly fast, and kill even quicker. They are also incredibly strong and sometimes pose too much of a threat for Kätekians, so most do their best to avoid areas where they roam.

Once everyone was settled inside, the driver of the carriage cracked a whip and the Guepusus took off at lightning speed, barreling through the hills and valleys in route to my final destination, the capital city: The Spire.

†††

After miles and miles of traveling, we finally reached The Spire. The carriage parked outside of the capital gates where Piaras—along with the others—exited. He opened up the cage and snatched me out, tossing me to the ground. He put one of his muddy and rain-drenched boots on the side of my face and proceeded to mash my head into a puddle on the cold asphalt.

"Well Aetherphile, here's where you meet your end. I tried to give you a chance to repent, but you didn't take it. Hope you're happy."

With half of my face submerged, all I could manage as a response were a few broken words and a lot of gurgling.

"Ah, it appears the cat's got his tongue," laughed one of the other Im-Ags. "You don't reckon we should just end him right here, do you?"

"No," an unfamiliar voice replied. "We want him alive. Can't you lot ever follow orders?"

The voice came from a slender man of average height with chalk-white skin and long-flowing, deep-red hair. He had animalistic, ruby-red eyes that glistened in the bright moonlight and was swathed in a lengthy and extravagant robe, underneath which he wore a white suit. Anybody could see from one glance that he was a man of status, but what was most interesting is the aura he projected. While not physically imposing, he just reeked of danger and malevolence. His mere presence promoted caution, though I wasn't sure why.

"That's enough, Piaras!" The Red-Headed Man commanded as he walked forward. "You always get carried away. Surely it wouldn't kill you to develop some restraint? You're an Imperial Agonizer, not a savage."

Piaras became shaken, which I would have never thought possible. Yet, at the words of this man, he wasted no time in removing his boot from my face.

"I apologize, my liege. But might I ask, why are you showing him mercy? I assume that Nosphero has been informed that he refused to repent. Clearly this freak doesn't deserve a measure of kindness."

"He deserves whatever the Alphacrats decide on. Now get him off the ground and bring him inside. He's due at the Citadel."

Piaras hurriedly bows. "As you wish, my liege."

***

Once inside the gates, I was "greeted" again, but this time by civilians.

And when I say "greeted", I mean that I was assailed with rocks, fruit and vegetables by a gauntlet of angry Vampires. They all lined the streets, screaming obscenities and threats as we headed towards the Citadel.

"Kill him! Kill the Aetherphile!" yelled one Vampire with a gruff and masculine voice.

"I hope you rot in Hell, you perverted scum!" went another, this time androgynous and rather elderly, but still strong. They possessed a bitterness in their voice which felt like it reverberated through me.

(Jesus, I knew the Vampires hated me, but not like this.)

More regret and remorse is starting to set in, yet I still refuse to repent. I don't want forgiveness, I don't want mercy and I damn sure don't want this shit to be prolonged. I just want to die. Quickly. I've been choked and beaten half to death, drained of my blood for weeks and now I'm being cursed at and assaulted by townies who are truthfully scared of me. They are only violent now because they know I'm weak. In any other event, I'd be ripping their hearts out or draining them of all their blood, but not before I made them all quake something fierce.

We were almost at the Citadel, when a little girl wearing a nun's habit and standing about as high as my waist, asked to give me a hug. It truly came as a shock, but The Red-Headed Man obliged her.

Piaras forced me onto my knees so that she could embrace me. Once she was close enough, she wrapped her arms around my neck and whispered in my ear, "May there never be mercy on your soul, you malignant piece of shit."

The little girl swiftly kicked me in my testicles and screamed, "There's no love for your kind, sinner! Respect the Covenant!"

She made a motion to kick me again, but The Red-Headed Man grabbed her by the back of her head and tossed her away like a paper ball towards an angry mob of about five people. The little runt screamed as she went hurtling into them. They all fell over from the force of her impact. It was at this point that I could see why Piaras was so shaken.

"Alright you savages, listen up!" The Red-Headed Man firmly commanded. "There will be no more attacking this fellow! If another of you lot dares to step forward and strike him, I will decapitate you with one flick! Don't believe me? Well be my guest and come at him!"

Before he could even finish issuing the challenge, another of the virulent townies attempted to assault me, but the poor sap never even got close.

He had barely dashed past The Red-Headed Man when, in the blink of an eye, he lost his head in a most gruesome display that made blood rain all over us and the crowd nearby.

"Thank you for volunteering," said The Red-Headed Man to the guy's head as he picked it up. "I wonder will others follow your lead?"

He kissed the decapitated head on the cheek and tossed it at the crowd, who dispersed as quick as a wink. I'd never seen anyone haul ass like that before. It was kind of humorous.

"Piaras, help him up please. You may have to carry him the rest of the way, doubt he can walk now."

He was right, I couldn't. Hell, I could barely stand. Being kicked in the balls had never hurt this much before, but being weakened prevented any kind of resistance I would have had against such an attack.

Piaras grunted, but heeded the orders given to him.

"Yes, my liege. As you wish."

I whispered to Piaras as he picked me up, "You've said that phrase a lot, are you hypnotized?"

"Young man, I'm loyal to the aristocracy." he replied, throwing me over his shoulder. "It is not hypnosis, only respect. If you had any sense of gratitude, you'd understand not to bite the hand that feeds you."

"There's never been a hand for me. I feed myself."

Piaras growled. "Sure you do, Otieno. Sure you do."

†††

Once we reached the front gate of the Citadel, Piaras placed me on the chilly and rain-soaked ground.

Directly in front of us stood Alphacrat Nosphero, staring with his crescent-shaped, steel-blue eyes as his shoulder-length, tousled ash-blonde hair flickered in the night's breeze. He was dressed in his purple and gold robe, while on his feet he wore a pair of velvet house slippers. Curious things to be wearing on a night such as this. It appeared he had been waiting for us since news of our arrival.

"Ah, my dear brother, you've finally made it," Nosphero gleefully expressed. "Glad to see you—and the 'cargo'—are in one piece."

"Indeed we are, big brother." replied Piaras, humbled by Nosphero's presence. "Are you surprised?"

"No no, not at all," —Nosphero folded his hands, as if to pray, but just put them under his chin— "but I must admit, I had my doubts that you'd bring him back alive."

"Well...to be honest...I really wanted to kill him, but I obeyed my orders. The mission comes first."

"Yes yes, it does, but did you have to beat him half to death before doing so?" asked Nosphero, frowning as he examined my bruised and battered condition.

"Surely you aren't upset, brother, especially after what he did?"

"He's a prisoner, Piaras, not a slave. And you're a man of nobility. You disgrace the name 'Tor' when you stoop to such actions."

"It seems more of a disgrace to go so light on this freak," scoffed Piaras.

"While there is no excuse for what this young boy did, there also isn't any excuse for the ones who murdered his love, even if she was an Aetherkind. Justice may be blind, but it is also fair."

"I guess," shrugged Piaras. "He's here now though, alive and–somewhat-well. What are your plans?"

Nosphero turned around and unlocked the gate. "Just take him inside, you'll find out soon enough."

Piaras went to grab my arm when suddenly there was a giant explosion that made the entire area rumble.

"What the—?!"

One of the Im-Ags made a gesture towards the Citadel, where there was a giant crater with thick, black smoke billowing from it.

"Ready the troops!" yelled Nosphero. "We're under attack!"

All at once, several large beams of white-hot light rained down from the sky, crashing into the ground like meteors. Piaras and Nosphero tumbled over, heaving and wheezing from the smoke blanketing the area. Amidst the distress and confusion, I managed to make out the silhouette of a svelte figure with wings coming through the smoke, brandishing a sword. When the figure came closer, I realized it was a woman. An Aetherkind—to be more precise—wearing a full suit of armor, which left only her eyes visible. While I couldn't recognize her based on eyes alone, something about her seemed oddly familiar.

As she made her way towards us, Nosphero started to rise to his feet.

"Whoever you are, I demand you stop this instant! I am Nosphero T—"

He was cut off mid sentence as she had decapitated him, his head soaring and spraying Piaras and I with blood along the way.

"You wretched bitch!" Piaras thundered. He lunged at her in a frenzied blitz but missed as she switfly sidestepped.

The Woman spread her wings and jetted high into the air, coming back down with a kick so mighty that it knocked the wind out of him. And being the big mountain of a tyrant that he is, Piaras hit the ground with a titanic rumble, landing flat on his back.

"You disgust me," The Woman said with a muffled voice, raising her sword.

"And your kind," Piaras spit out the blood filling his mouth. "have always disgusted me......Wicked whore."

With both hands clasped firmly on it, the woman brought the sword down, thrusting it into Piaras forehead. He convulsed then shortly succumbed to death. After killing him, she turned her attention to me.

"Please!" I howled with my hands in the air. "I don't want any trouble! Whatever your quarrel is with them, I am COMPLETELY bereft of responsibility."

I shocked myself with how I reacted, as I don't know why I wanted to live so bad at that moment. I guess that it was less of me wanting to live and more of not wanting to be slain for the crimes of those aristocratic fools. Still, something in me had changed instantly, and I no longer desired death. With my hands still in the air, I pleaded once more.

"Miss... I am begging you... please... do not kill me."

The Woman giggled, then removed her helmet.

"I'm not here to kill you, Otieno."

With the helmet removed her voice was clearer, as was her face, but when I saw it, I couldn't believe my eyes.

"Cantrelle? You're alive?!"

>>> TO BE CONTINUED <<<

JADA SHERFFIELD

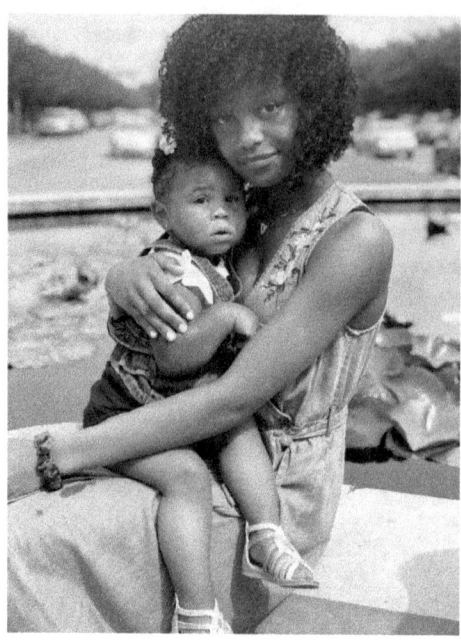

As a writer for the reckoning, I wish to find my creative voice. I'd like to be a journalist someday, but I have to first find my voice and identify the issues I feel most passionate about. I'm happy to have the opportunity because it allows me to write about personal topics, and feel inspired by the many other writers on the website. I hope to be relatable enough to convey my feelings in a meaningful way, but also to show how acknowledging differing perspectives can bring people closer. I want to be a better storyteller. To improve my skills so that i'm better at emphasizing my emotions and organizing them.

Can I Identify?

As a young black woman, (not in poverty, not in economic distress, not oppressed - privileged) I feel like my emotions are uncalled for and unjust (I do not have the right to say I struggle emotionally, when in reality, most people struggle to identify with the specifics of the circumstances I face.

Which provokes thought in me, are they wrong or am I just sensitive? And may I be? Seeing as I've never experienced direct racism of any kind, never witnessed police brutality, have no trouble in stores, and am rarely called out of my name. Consistency is an expectation when your actions say so. So, if I'm not constantly experiencing discrimination is it okay for me to identify with someone who does because we have the same skin? Can I call myself a victim?

I acknowledge my privilege, I struggle to understand how to use my voice for the African Americans community when I struggle to personally relate to some of the hardships. There is a deep emptiness in me that wants to be filled with the history, resiliency and culture of my people. I'm yearning to know more.

Our often appropriated culture is hard to defend when I can't always identify with it. There are several young black women out there confused just like me. Movements such as #MeToo and #BlackLivesMatter inspire me, but is there a cause I can really speak to, when I haven't personally been sexually harassed or discriminated against. Firsthand accounts of my life aren't being published in newspapers and shown on the news. Headlines like privilege black girl playing FortNite on iPhone 11 don't pop up because they're insignificant to the cause. But, perhaps Breonna Taylor struggled to relate as well. Perhaps she made straight A's and spoke "proper".

I am not rushed for a relatable experience but I am angry and hurt and in disbelief. I still know that my lack of experience in racial discrimination today does not exempt me from the harsh reality that I can be Breonna Taylor and George Floyd tomorrow. Black people will mourn my death while others try to find the hiccups in my privileged life to justify a discriminatory death.

The complexity of my reality and the knowledge of the truth - burdens me. Why can't my reality be my truth? Lack of personal experience or not I am not naive, I know that Breonna Taylor could easily be me. But, who do I speak for when I can't relate?

Young Prejudice

I've always known that I'm naturally introverted. Though sometimes I'm proud of this characteristic because I have become more observant, often my silence is misinterpreted as weakness. For 2-3 years in elementary school, my peers manipulated and mocked me (and some teachers) and in one instance, even physically assaulted.

On that day, the gym teacher separated the class into teams and told us to find team mats. My team went to a mat and sat down. One girl in my grade and I were struggling to get along. She had been at the school for 5 years and I had recently moved to Tennessee with my family in third grade. She was white, had plenty of friends and we were constantly in competition with one another. Some of my teachers were identifying me as a leader and it sparked a conflict between the two of us. The "title" I held which she felt rightfully belonged to her. She walked over to my team mat and wanted it for her team.

The rest of my teammates instantly looked for another mat. I debated the matter. This suddenly became a test of dominance. After a few moments of name-calling, I believe she understood that I would not move from the space-based solely on her demand and she slapped me across my face. I paused for a moment, partly in disbelief and partly because everyone looked away. No one came to my defense. I finally left the mat but only to inform a teacher of what had happened. I wish I could tell you that the teacher believed me or maybe after the school did a small investigation, and I received an apology. Instead, I was called to the office and although witnesses confirmed that she hit me; it made me feel as if it was my fault. My unwillingness to speak about it affected the way I interacted with people for years afterward.

Yes, it's shocking that a little girl who slapped me in the face in 4th grade could have left a mark when it came to my relationships with people. But, it set a precedent for how I was to be treated by my white females classmates. There were several other occurrences where similar behaviors were exhibited from other classmates even from other schools.

Before this, I was quiet but full of thought. I wanted to feel like I belonged so it wasn't uncommon for me to have meaningful conversations with the few who appreciated me, some of which had to witness the name-calling, gossip, and foul play they exposed me to. I spoke my mind and was labeled as "less than" because of it. There are times knowing well enough that I could have spoken up, I didn't, and that allowed them to take advantage of me and the reputation I had created for myself. My peers maneuvered me into situations just to embarrass me. By the end of it I was so belittled in confidence and assertiveness I let the bias dictate the way I performed. I struggled with an open expression because I didn't feel entitled to loving myself.

Everytime I moved something similar to fourth grade happened. Over and over again until I successfully learned to suppress my emotions. I spoke less, studied more, and enjoyed myself in silence. My parents were not involved as much as they might have wanted to be at this point in my life. One was deployed, and the other was balancing raising my sisters and managing a household. The community I came home to frequently left me with the option to be alone, which is why I turned to writing. I would write poems and song lyrics to contemplate on the way they treated me.

While I may have overcome the environment I was in, I still suffered the effects long after. Every day felt like a flashback of a nightmare. Stuck in my old routine of retreating to my room. Until November 2018, my step father spoke to me and said, "You have to trust me, that's what parents are for." He explained to me he saw how I struggled and I was not alone. He talked about his responsibility to be my outlet when my mother isn't home or when

I'm in distress. During that conversation I broke down into a fit of tears. I realized that's all I ever wanted to hear, and amidst the tears I finally felt worthy of love, worthy of an opinion, and worthy of a voice. So, I encourage black women to be there for each other. Be aware of what your sister and sometimes brother are going through.

PARIS TAYLOR

Andromeda

She feels like home. A reference points
Cemented in the north star
an anchor of genealogy
generations can be formed in our hugs
I can trace her smell for miles
Like home; Soft
But only for those who know her creaks
Hard; But only for those who don't
I use to know her blueprints by heart.
Now some pathways I've lost
Forgotten-- keys given away
But the doorbell still tolls for me
And standing outside right now
She feels like home
I don't even have to knock

Water Falls from the clouds

I fall asleep to thunderstorms
To raindrops finding their way home
Everybody is afraid of being lost
Lightning acts as street lamps
"Its bout time to come inside"
And thunder always follows behind
Like a personal orchestra
Or a marching band
Or this playlist
And If I were to fall in love with every note?
There would still be room for you.

On Being Colored

She said, "Write our love on pages of white!"

the margins ate it – how funny is theft?

In a world of grey, only color is left.

Ask the sky, she begs for color, fights

With ocean blues, bleeding red, til black as night.

This is the nature of love unprofessed:

The most beautiful love, a soft caress.

Did she know color falls outside their sight?

Your love shined gold, fitting me like a glove

Yet, they call it rainbow. I ask, "Mister,

Why don't we ever see those precious doves,

White as day, that tell me I can kiss her?"

        How queer—like when I proclaim "She is my love!"

        And everybody thinks we are sisters.

Aren't I someone?
I am always 2 rivers, 2 paths, 2 choices,
And you want me to take
"the road less travelled"
That's why I always lose one shoe
Throw my keys strangers
Drown my thoughts in lakes
And only take left turns
I am still here.